STYLE IS ETERNAL

STYLE IS ETERNAL

NICOLE JENKINS

MELBOURNE UNIVERSITY PUBLISHING
An imprint of Melbourne University Publishing Limited
Level 1, 11–15 Argyle Place South,
Carlton, Victoria 3053, Australia
mup-info@unimelb.edu.au
www.mup.com.au

Cover and text design by Trisha Garner
Cover images kindly supplied by Dominique Janssen
 at TopVintage (topvintage.nl/en)
Cover photography by Alice Primowees
Model photography by Dominic Deacon
 (www.42ndstreetphotography.com.au)

Printed in China by 1010 Printing International Limited

National Library of Australia Cataloguing-in
-Publication entry

Jenkins, Nicole, author.
Style is eternal/Nicole Jenkins.
9780522866407 (paperback)
Fashion.

Clothing and dress.
Dress accessories.
Self-presentation.

646.3

*For Rebekah and Victoria, the women who have inspired me —
and for everyone who has felt the power of a good frock.*

Fashion fades ... style is eternal

YVES SAINT LAURENT

PREFACE

ashion fascinates me. All my life I have striven to dress well, and I'm often asked for advice by others who are grappling with fashion rules or just feel like they could get a little more from their wardrobes.

It wasn't always this way: my childhood involved lots of moving around. I had a succession of homes and schools, and the more new schools there were, the shyer I became. This wasn't helped by the old clothes that my mum dressed me in. Our family loved antiques and history, so I had a vintage look ahead of my time, but what was cool in North Sydney exposed me to bullying in South Perth.

I just wanted to fit in, but my attempts always failed—I had to accept that I just wasn't like the other girls. I needed to dress to my own tune.

After a brief foray into modern fashion, a new age dawned when I rediscovered vintage, aged fifteen. One wonderful day I spotted a polka-dot party dress hanging high above the racks in an op shop, and for the princely sum of eight dollars I gave it a happy home. With this new treasure I let go of my awkward attempts to follow mainstream fashion and embraced being a creative dresser.

It hasn't been easy—the good people of Perth went out of their way to tell me what they thought of my unorthodox fashion choices, but I soon learnt that feeling like 'me' was infinitely more valuable than pleasing the masses—an impossible task anyway.

I flounced my way through my teens in full-skirted, floral dresses with petticoats and seamed stockings, sashayed through my early twenties in fitted, lace cocktail dresses and stilettos, and landed in wintery London, aged twenty-six, looking for work in film as an art director. Instead, I landed a job at a French fashion house.

Along the way I had studied costume design, run a vintage clothing boutique and worked in theatre, but my new job—and the inclement weather—saw me incorporate current fashion into my wardrobe once again. A confirmed frock lover, I even started to wear trousers for the first time in my life.

Over the next decade I mixed current trends with vintage to my sartorial advantage. And when I'd cracked the code, I set up my own boutique in 2004, called Circa Vintage Clothing, through which I've been fortunate enough to dress all kinds of interesting people from all around the world, including Dita von Teese, Florence Welch and Amanda Palmer.

I hope through this book to demystify the age-old fashion rules and inspire you, so that you can break them and make them your own. I'll walk you through analysing your wardrobe to make it better and help you have fun with different looks from all eras. You will find the tools you need to take charge of your choices and see beyond limited 'High Street' fashion to find new ideas in unexpected places.

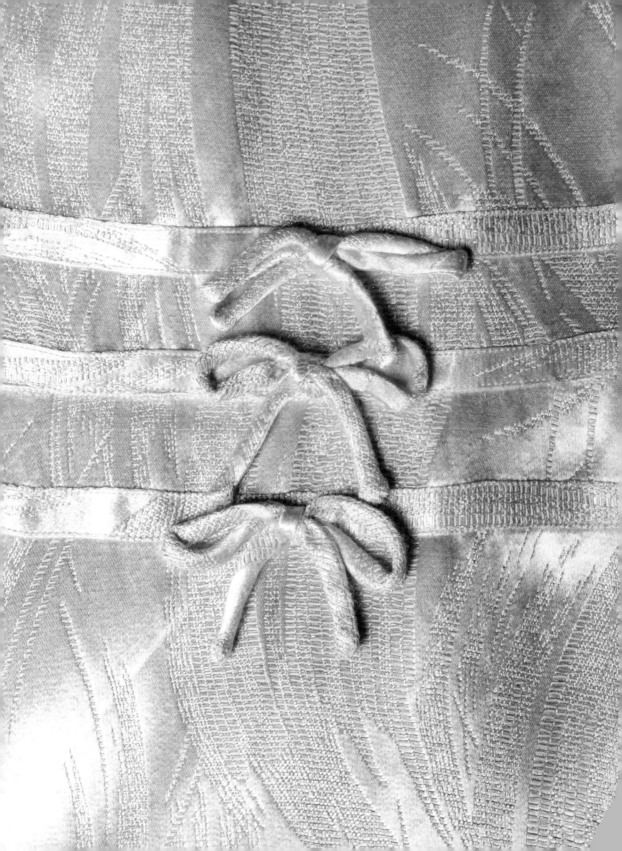

FASHION FADES

Ruffled collar

Fashion is a reflection of the society that wears it. It is always the first element to change during cultural shifts—think short skirts in the 1960s and the sexual revolution—but it's also innately personal. It speaks volumes about the needs and wants of the wearer.

The business of fashion is about creating desire and selling clothes—competing to offer the trendiest, most up-to-the-minute styles. Trend creation is a constantly renewing cycle, so you need to buy more to keep up as well as top up with items that work with what you already have.

This vortex, along with the historical association of fashion as a 'women's interest', has contributed to a feeling that fashion is a shallow and trivial matter, not worthy of serious consideration.

Fashion, for me, is a form of wearable art. Functional, everyday items that serve practical purposes but contain the capacity to inspire and delight.

Keeping up with fashion is serious work—people watching, magazine and blog reading, plus shopping. Not to mention the financial investment required, often for something that will soon look 'out of date'. While they may briefly reflect the zeitgeist, not all fashions stick, and the less flattering ones invariably pass quickly.

The fashion world changed significantly during the 1990s, when developing countries began offering far cheaper mass production and 'fast fashion' took hold; suddenly a new look could transition from design to finished garment on the rack within a fortnight, enabling a continuous flow of new styles. This speed inspired retail staff to push products, and the customer soon learned that time is of the essence. Fast fashion was much cheaper than traditional retail too, which also contributed to booming sales.

The fast-fashion model that we now know so well can utilise small production runs, meaning there is less investment at stake in any individual style. A successful style can always be produced again quickly, although it is often the case that by then the trends have already moved on.

The downside to low-cost, offshore production is that developing countries often don't provide the worker protections and provisions that we take for granted. More cost savings are produced by reducing the quality of fabric and construction.

Poor-quality garments result in increasing waste and an environmental toll—the average cotton t-shirt will be worn and washed around twenty times before becoming landfill. Even more alarming is the widespread use of synthetic materials that are not biodegradable and have few recycling options, unlike the cotton t-shirt, which can be made or reconstituted into something else.

Each season there will be the highly visible, 'on-trend' items that are usually bright, unusually coloured, or nice and shiny with metallic foils or bling. They might be uncommon or bold shapes. They are deliberately eye-catching because they're the bait to entice you into the shop or webstore.

Only the bravest will buy the on-trend items, but their numbers are sufficient to ensure the success of the trend and attract others to the brand. The fashion labels appreciate that most of us are less courageous and will buy the same things we always do: the black and neutral basics that help us fit in at work and with our peers, at best with some statement accessories.

Basics are useful, and can be good building blocks of a functional wardrobe, but they're not inspiring and will rarely feed your hungry sartorial soul, even for those who aren't looking to stand out. They shouldn't form the entirety of your wardrobe. We all want to add a touch of individuality.

Go beyond basics, classics and trends to translate fashion into a style that works for you. This is what I'd love to help you achieve—how to dress to suit your personality, lifestyle and shape, and how to rise above the endless cycle of buying new clothes or wearing boring old ones, and save money and wardrobe space too!

By culling unwanted items from your wardrobe and adapting others that have potential, you can then address any gaps by adding considered pieces, sourced from a variety of origins. Broaden your style horizons and open up unlimited options and outfit combinations.

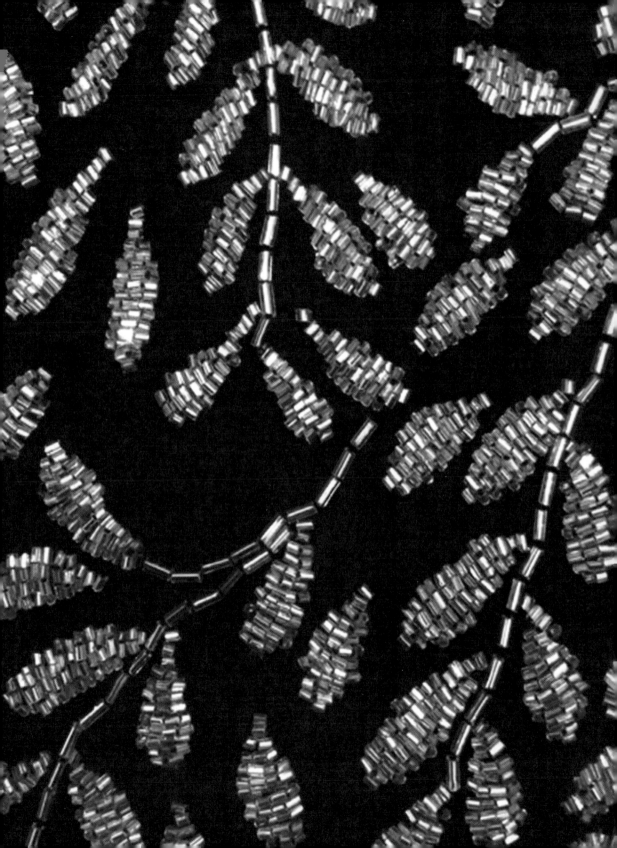

STYLE IS ETERNAL

You are unique, and your wardrobe, as much as other spheres of your life, can be a celebration of your individuality and you-ness. How you present yourself is something that deserves some consideration.

Your wardrobe might reflect the values of your peer group or your occupation, but there will be pieces that are less predictable. Maybe you wear your grandmother's ring or a t-shirt that you printed in art class.

Even in the most classic of wardrobes, there is always a little wiggle room to introduce personal touches, perhaps something vintage or a piece with nostalgic beauty. I would encourage this as a first step. Soon, you'll find that you're comfortable with more.

Some people work with their own particular tastes, others look to different role models and icons for inspiration. Style is about who you are and what works for you at this point of your life; your style will need updating as your life changes. As we age our body shapes, occupations and lifestyles change—these all demand style adaptations.

You might be among the creative people who are able to change styles every day like a chameleon, depending on mood or social context, or you might work on developing a signature style that reflects your particular aesthetic. But a warning: signature looks can be a boon or a millstone; make sure that it works to your advantage and re-evaluate and update it when your needs change.

Chameleons will find that their wardrobes can match the pace of their life, with each change reflected in their look. It's a way to feel as if you're defining each and every moment in time. If this is you, consider taking plenty of photos, as you may want a record of these different manifestations of yourself in the future.

Style can be a snug blanket to wrap around you to protect you from the world. What you wear influences your relationships with your friends, family, colleagues and the general public. It can intimidate and keep them at a distance or it can encourage people to warm to you by expressing a friendly and approachable air.

Stylish people make the world better for all of us. They can be like moving artworks, challenging our ways of thinking about dressing and creating beauty. They don't need to be famous: the anonymous, fabulously dressed person going about their business is a wonderful and life-affirming thing. If you wish to express to them how they've brightened up your day a smile will often suffice. We should celebrate these people for their contribution to our cultural life. Their influence will outlast them and remain forever inspiring.

STYLE ESSENTIALS

Full skirt

To make the most of your wardrobe, you need to discover not only what you already have, but also what is possible and how to go beyond your current limits.

Regular fashion retail will present certain limited options, but there are many ways to get what you want: try retailers that cater to different markets, age groups, cultural groups or the opposite gender. Look at small, specialist shops like those that stock horse-riding gear or work boots for tradespeople. Try online shops locally and abroad, and second-hand and vintage shops. Never have we been presented with such a variety of accessible choices.

Fashion can also be adapted and updated, or designed and constructed, by you or a friendly dressmaker. There are no limits to what you can buy and change.

Creativity is key. Start with the first building block—a dress, top and bottom or a one-piece (onesie). Over this you might add a jacket or coat for warmth or style. Then accessorise—with extras that can be either functional (hats, scarves, bags), decorative (jewellery), or both.

Let's look at some of the possibilities.

DRESSES

I truly believe there is no better garment for a woman than the dress—the simplicity of one piece that you can dress up or down as you wish. A dress is instantly transforming: it contains the power of the feminine.

I once had fifty 1950s dresses that were hung from the picture rails in my Art Deco flat, like big fabric flowers, and each morning I would select the one to wear that day. They were much admired—both hanging and when I wore them.

Someone once asked to select my gown for a party one night, a potent suggestion that I accepted—and later he became my boyfriend. Another fellow felt intimidated by a slinky, velvet cocktail frock I wore for a dinner date: I should have realised then that he wasn't the one for me. Dresses, and the reaction they garner can tell you so much.

The right dress, which flatters your height, figure and age, always wins out for me over any other fashion choice.

Dresses are the traditional female garment from babyhood to old age. Women in every era have worn dresses, and it's easy to understand why. Dresses are so great that men have gotten in on the act at times—in hot countries and for some occupations, like the clergy.

Dresses fell out of favour in the 1960s with a shift in fashion to youthful styles—where previously ladies had looked forward to turning thirty so that they could wear the elegant, glamorous styles of the grown woman, now it was all about being young and vigorous, and part of this was a return to the styles of childhood—less formal separates like jeans and t-shirts came into vogue with 'mix and match'.

The idea was that you could have a more versatile wardrobe by putting combinations together to create new looks. It was a con—women were dressing like infants and missing out on the powerful expression of femininity that is innate in the dress.

ever completely went away of course: in the 1960s there were cute little A-line shifts modelled on 1920s styles; the 1970s looked back to nineteenth-century fashions with Laura Ashley cotton-print maxi dresses, and the 1980s was all about ruched, polyester party dresses with liberal sprinklings of beads and sequins. For most of us now dresses are 'dressy'—best worn for special occasions like weddings and the races, events that hark back to bygone days of glamour and elegance. And that's wonderful, but a dress can be more than that. It can be casual and practical, perfect for sport or travel as well as shopping and picnics.

What makes a dress 'dressy' is the fabric—luxury materials like satins, laces and velvets have traditionally been worn for important occasions. A 'dressy' dress is often more structured and features a plain colour rather than a print—the preserve of the day dress—and might be embellished with detailing like beading, embroidery, appliqués or sequins.

BALLGOWN

COAT DRESS

COCKTAIL

DAY

DEBUTANTE

ENSEMBLE

HOUSECOAT
OR HOUSEDRESS

PARTY, FORMAL
OR PROM

DRESS STYLES

BALLGOWN—the most formal of dresses, also suitable for red carpet events and for the unorthodox bride. Floor length and either of rich fabrics or heavily embellished. Tiaras, gloves and sparkly jewellery and accessories will ramp up the glamour. The men are likely to be wearing black or white tie, so all stops are out!

COAT DRESS—a day dress in the style of a coat. Can be worn as either garment, but generally as a dress; looks nice with a petticoat underneath.

COCKTAIL—understated elegance, a well-fitted dress that shows off a woman's charms without the megaphone. Hems are around knee length and dark colours are best—gloves get extra points, especially if the wearer is sipping a martini. Small veiled hats and hair ornaments go a long way. Sophisticated femininity at its best.

DAY—dresses for comfort and practicality, not neglecting charm. Simple, colourful shifts with cardigans, or sweet florals with full skirts—all casual styles are great for the daytime. That said, with the right attitude you can pull off a dressy number in the day too.

DEBUTANTE—a sweeter, younger, whiter take on the wedding gown for teenagers at their first 'presentation'.

ENSEMBLE—a dress with a matching jacket of the same fabric. Popular in the 1930s and 1960s, ensembles are a smart way to dress for dressy day occasions like the races or weddings.

HOUSECOAT OR HOUSEDRESS— traditionally worn by housewives and practical enough to be washed easily and cover marks but fancy enough to greet the plumber or do a little local grocery shopping. Identifying features are easy removal (centre-front zippers, big buttons) and generously sized pockets, often on the front so small items can be easily tucked away while doing the laundry.

PARTY, FORMAL OR PROM—fun and fancy frocks are often in bright or pastel colours. Fabrics include satin, tulle and chiffon. Silhouettes are generally fitted or full skirted to emphasise a woman's form. Worn with high heels, a little jewellery and a winning smile.

DRESS SILHOUETTES FOR ALL FIGURES

A-LINE—introduced by couturier Christian Dior in 1955, the style flows out in a triangular shape from the shoulders, so the waist is wider than the bust and the hips wider still. An antidote to the waist-fixated styles of the time, it came into its own in the 1960s and has been with us since. It suits those with pear shapes or larger waists.

BIAS CUT—introduced by couturier Madeleine Vionnet in the 1930s, the fabric of the dress is cut on the bias (diagonally, instead of along the weft threads), producing natural stretch and nice draping. The result works best for slim ladies with soft curves but less well for the voluptuous, as the clinging fabric has a tendency to emphasise roundness. Wearing a petticoat underneath helps smooth out lumps and bumps.

DROP-WAISTED—introduced in the 1920s, the bust and waist is usually a tube flowing to the hips, where there are either pleats, flares, gathers or inserts for movement. Sashes or detailing might further highlight the hips. Original 1920s versions are also flat-chested

in the fashion of the time. Modern versions add bust shaping and sometimes waist shaping too, although the hips remain the focal point. Styles are good for ladies with slim hips, great legs, small busts or thick waists.

EMPIRE LINE—a very high waist, which sits just under the bust. An early-nineteenth-century style lends height to a shorter woman, emphasises the bust and distracts from broad hips or a thick waist.

FITTED, PENCIL OR WIGGLE—a dress that is shaped to a woman's body. Best for ladies with slim or hourglass figures. Especially good for highlighting a slim waist or hips and excellent for a large-busted woman who is slim elsewhere.

MAXI—the skirt hem is ankle length. Full-length dresses that hide the legs often reveal something else to compensate, so feature halter necks, a plunging neckline or bare arms and best suit women who like showing off these attributes. Also good for those of us who are shy about our legs.

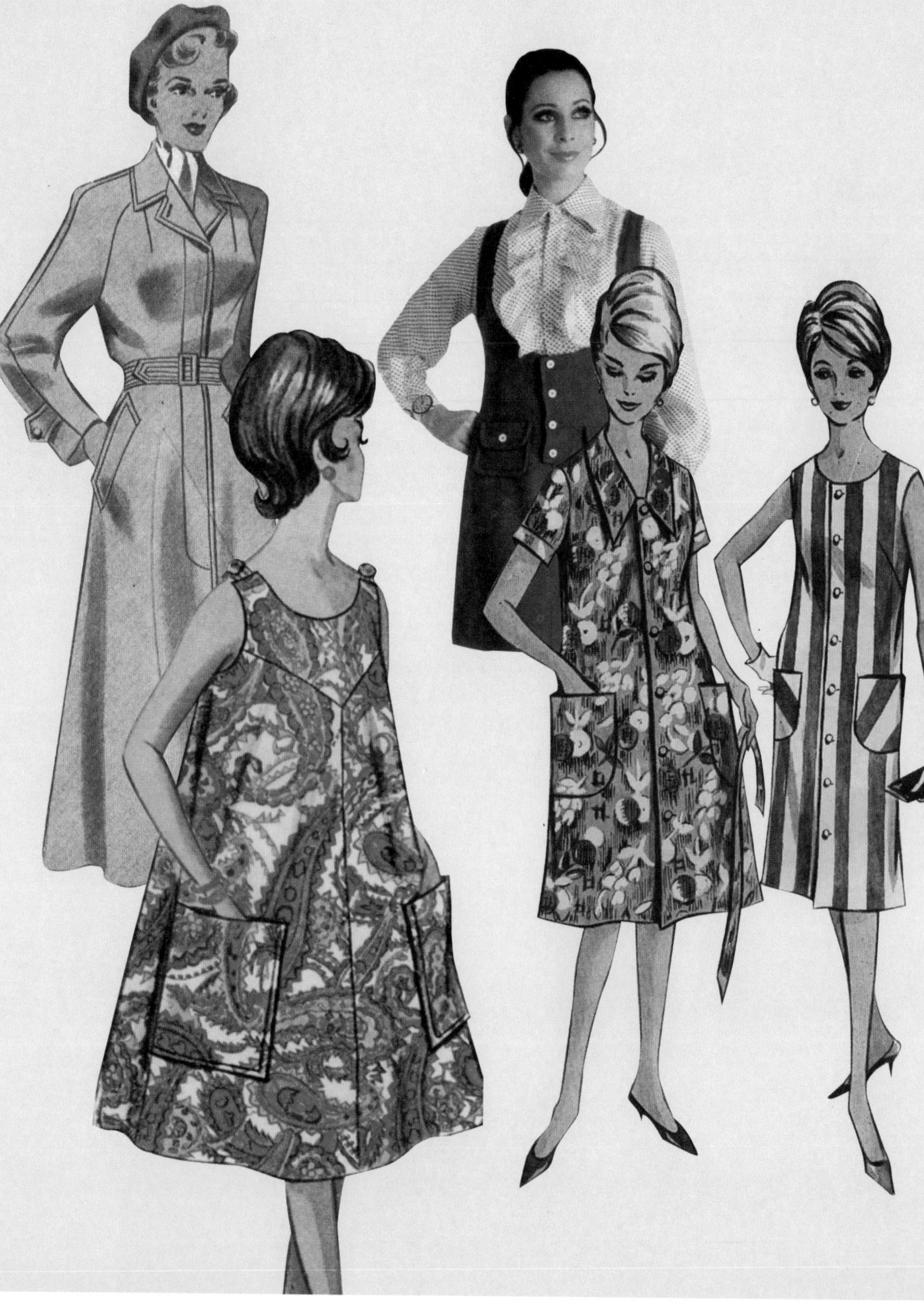

MINI—the skirt hem is above the knees. The best style for women blessed with great legs. How short exactly will depend on how confident you are of your legs (and your underwear!), but one way to tone it down is to wear opaque or patterned hosiery. Works really well with knee-high boots.

PINAFORE—an overdress, worn over a top or jumper. A great style for colder months, reminiscent of playful girlish styles but smart enough for the office in tailored versions.

PRINCESS LINE (fit and flare)—features shaping into the waist with vertical seams, without a horizontal waist seam, elongating the body, adding height and emphasising curves. Best for hourglass figures where curvy hips accentuate a small waist.

SARONG—influenced by Eastern styles of dress, with a side drape and either a wrap or a faux wrap. A touch of exoticism, sarongs work well for slim figures, especially if they are strapless or offer little bust support.

SHIFT—plainly cut dress with little variation in width from bust to hip. A fitted shift has shaping to the bust and waist and can be more flattering of womanly curves.

SHIRT DRESS OR SHIRTWAISTER—based on a shirt, featuring buttons down the front with short or long sleeves and a fitted or full skirt. It's definitely one for the daytime. This style keeps on coming back in, and there are options to flatter all figures.

SMOCK—originally worn as maternity wear or protection for artists painting. The smock features a yoked shoulder line and front opening with a simple body. Still a favourite for pregnancy and those with bellies. Not generally a very flattering style, but a shorter length can help.

SWING OR TRAPEZE—an extreme version of A-line where the skirt hem is significantly wider than the shoulders, flowing loosely. A style that works for women with broad hips and waists; can be unsightly if worn too long.

"Summer Breeze"

If this is the shade you require, tear off sample and send with order.

JUMPSUITS AND PLAYSUITS

The one-piece with trousers is a popular, if inevitably short-lived, recurring fashion. Best suited to very small children with their simple needs, adults soon tire of the craze due to the limitations of the design: the complications of going to the ladies' room and the fact that the bagginess needed from shoulder to crotch to make sitting down comfortable, is unattractive when standing up. Most people prefer a sleeker look.

But still, it's a fun alternative to dresses and separates. Due to their slouchy nature, jumpsuits and playsuits are best suited to casual occasions.

JUMPSUIT AND PLAYSUIT STYLES

BOILER SUIT—a sleeved version with centre-front zipper and elasticised waist, popular in the 1970s and based on industrial workwear. Generally of heavy cotton drill.

OVERALLS—the top features a bib held up by adjustable straps over the shoulders, to be worn over a t-shirt, shirt or bare chest. Also based on a workwear style.

PLAYSUIT—a young style worn by girls in the 1940s to 1960s and featuring shorts. Commonly in bright floral prints and gingham cottons, perhaps with a matching overskirt.

ONESIE—a hooded style worn by infants which has recently appeared in many styles for adults, including fun animal versions. All the body is covered and only the face exposed.

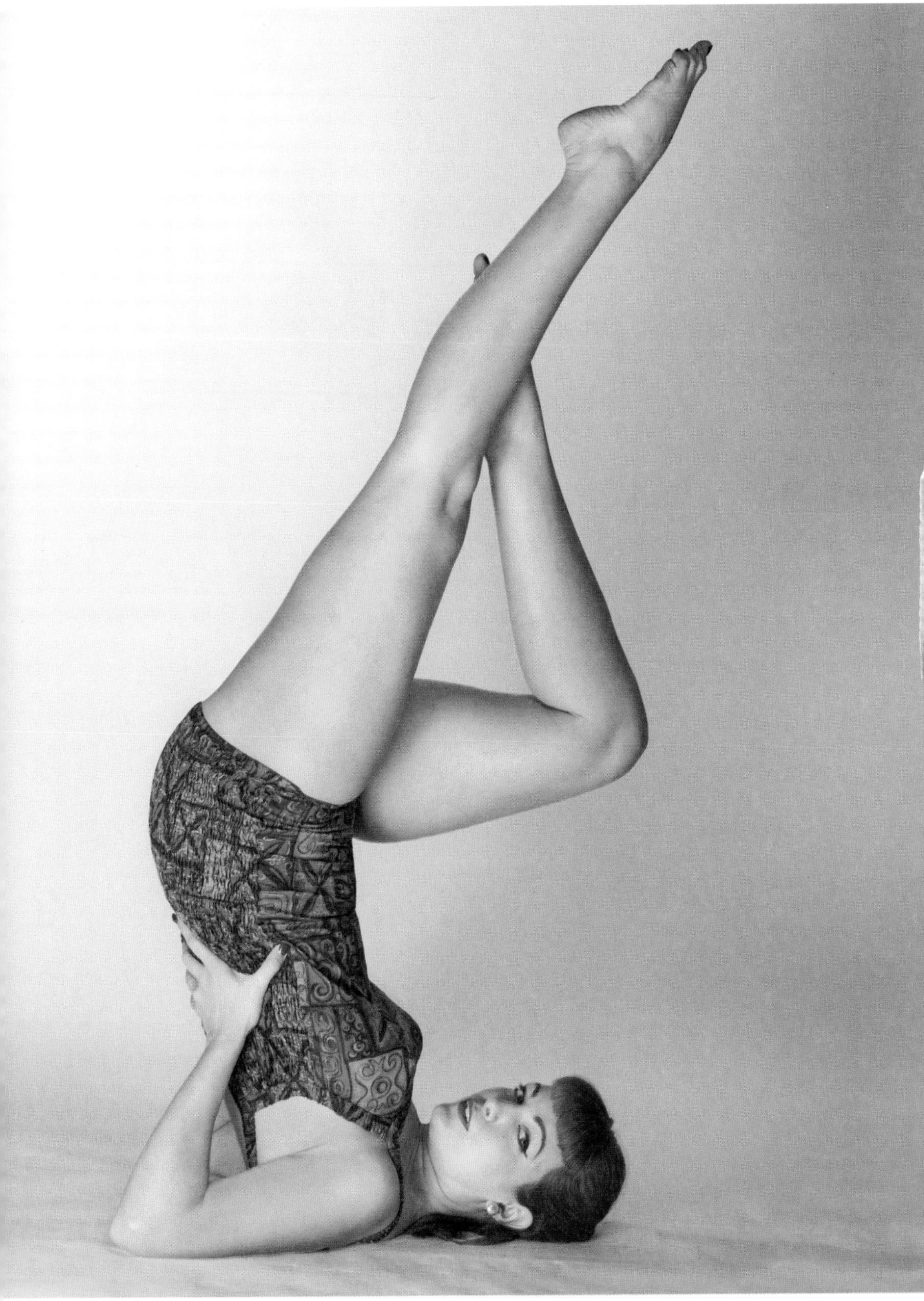

SEPARATES

Born out of menswear, ladies' separates were originally conceived as practical garments, best suited for hard work, sporting or casual occasions. As a result, separates have been the poor cousin of dresses for most of fashion history.

It was Coco Chanel who saw their potential in the early twentieth century and produced them in a range of fabrics, including silks. Most of the Western world was slow to catch on—the dress is hard to beat—but during the 1960s 'Youth-quake' tops and bottoms were celebrated by the teen market.

Since the 1970s, when it was all about 'this goes with that' and 'mix and match', separates have formed the majority of a woman's wardrobe, even for dressy occasions. It's quite common for women to wear separates to the exclusion of dresses.

Separates can also be worn in layers of tops and bottoms, for example, a tank top over a t-shirt or an open-front maxi skirt over hot pants. The many possible combinations offer a high degree of creativity and can be particularly useful when the weather changes, allowing the wearer to add, or peel off, a layer or two.

TOPS

Essentially, tops are the top half of dresses and come in the same kinds of varieties—they may or may not have sleeves and lengths and necklines vary. They might be made of any fabric, or even be sheer. Tops come in many styles including blouses, shirts, t-shirts, tank tops (singlets), midriff or crop tops and shell tops (sleeveless and fitted). Women's shirts and blouses with centre-front buttons will button right over left, to differentiate from menswear, which buttons left over right.

FROM
7'11

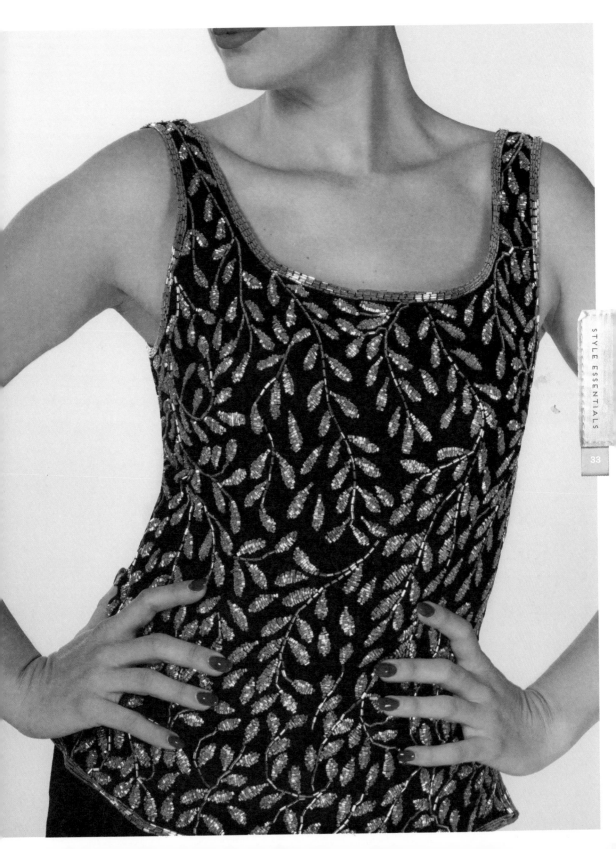

SKIRTS

Skirts also come in a variety of lengths and shapes and may have either feature pockets or hidden ones inserted into a seam. Pockets are a wonderful thing, and not often enough found in womenswear.

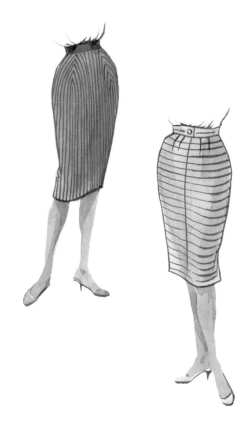

SKIRT STYLES

A-LINE—a triangular silhouette where the hem is greater than the hips and waist, but not as full as a flared skirt.

ASYMMETRIC—an uneven hem that is longer on one or more sides, for example, longer in the back than the front. A gimmick trend that can be evened up once the fashion has passed.

BUBBLE SKIRT—a double skirt, the over-skirt being voluminous and gathered into the hem of the under-skirt creating a bubble effect. Popular in the late 1950s and late 1980s, they can be converted into regular skirts by separating the two hems and ironing out the gathers.

CIRCLE SKIRT—almost universally flattering, but watch out for length: too long can be frumpy and age you (although a very long 'ballet length' skirt worn with a narrow waist can be very chic, especially with ballet flats or lace-up shoes), just as too short can be awkward when bending over. Medium lengths work best for most figures, although knee-length itself should generally be avoided as it has the effect of cutting the legs in half and exposing the knees—Christian Dior considered knees to be the least attractive part of a woman's body, and I'm inclined to agree.

FLARED—fullness in the skirt is fitted smoothly into the waist through vertical seams. These are available in several lengths from mini 'skater' to full-length maxi. Panels provide more shape, and a curved S seam produces a mermaid or tulip skirt.

FULL—a rectangular piece of fabric (generally 2–3 metres long) that is gathered along one length into a waistband. Popular in the 1950s to create the illusion of curvy hips for slim teenage figures, they suit women of all ages and are one of the easiest skirts to make, as they require no pattern. Note that they bulk out the waist, so are best in small sizes. One option is to replace the gathers with pleats, which sit flatter.

MAXI—a full-length or ankle-length skirt of any style.

MIDI—halfway between mini and maxi, the hem sits slightly below the knees.

MINI—any skirt with a hem that sits above the knee.

PENCIL OR STRAIGHT—fitted through the waist and hip, sometimes shaped down the legs too. This style needs to fit loosely enough at the hips and waist to enable sitting; a tight skirt might look more flattering, but it will quickly crease up. Fitted versions should have one or more kick pleats or splits/vents to enable movement. Long, straight skirts make excellent evening wear, and the most elegant styles have a centre-back vent. A variation is a long split to the thigh on one side of the front, Jessica Rabbit style.

WIGGLE SKIRT—similar to a pencil skirt but with a hem narrower than the hip, preventing free movement. The wearer is forced to walk slowly and 'wiggle' in an alluring but highly impractical manner. Their precursor was the short-lived Edwardian 'hobble skirt', whose narrowness covered an actual belt worn around the legs, constraining movement. The modern wiggle skirt shouldn't be so restrictive.

A NOTE ON PLEATS

Pleating is an elegant and efficient alternative to gathering—it creates minimal bulk and maximum freedom for movement.

A long length of fabric is folded repeatedly and the resulting pleats are embossed on the fabric through a heating process. Natural fibres have no 'memory', and so will lose their pleats when washed, whereas synthetic fibres retain their shape. Thus, most pleated garments will contain a synthetic component; if not, the pleats will need to be ironed back in after laundering or dry cleaning.

SOME TYPES OF PLEATS

KNIFE—a series of parallel pleats all going in the one direction. The width of the pleat may vary although all pleats will be equidistant. The most common type of pleats.

ACCORDION—a very fine set of knife pleats, generally used as a trim, especially on lingerie.

BOX—a pleat that is folded in one direction and then the opposite, so that it sits (box-like) inwards or outwards—most common is the inverted box pleat.

FORTUNY STYLE—a soft, crinkly pleat introduced by the designer Mariano Fortuny in the early twentieth century for his sumptuous silk column gowns, such as the iconic Delphos. The technique remains a mystery, but some modern designers have succeeded in producing a similar effect. Silk garments must be twisted into knots for storage or their pleats will fall out, while polyesters do not require special care.

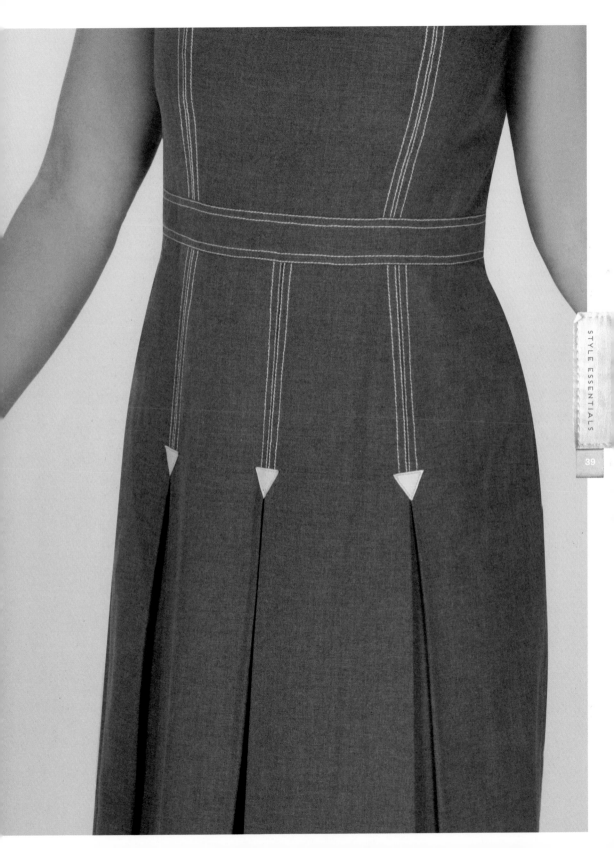

STYLE IS ETERNAL

40

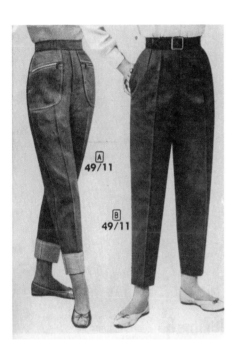

TROUSERS

From its humble beginning, women have embraced the trouser with great zeal, and it now forms the backbone of many wardrobes, from cotton denim jeans to silk jersey evening versions. As with many garments, they come in two main types: loose or fitted.

TROUSER STYLES

CIGARETTE OR STOVEPIPE—full-length fitted or tight pants, often with a side zipper so that the front sits untroubled by a fly. Fit is paramount here; underwear should be carefully chosen to avoid a visible panty line. Chic in black or plain colours or gingham.

CAPRI PANTS—similar to cigarette pants, but ending mid-calf, the perfect look for an Italian summer holiday with a sleeveless top and hair tied back with a silk scarf.

HAREM PANTS OR (MC) HAMMER PANTS—loose style often found in Eastern shops when not in fashion. Very comfortable, or so I've heard.

FLARES—high-waisted trousers with wide legs. Popularised during World War II, this style was revived big time in the 1970s and is flattering to curvy figures, as flares are especially good for showing off a nice waist-hip ratio or bum. The trouser legs fall gracefully from the hips, either at the same or greater width (very wide hemmed versions are called bell bottoms or elephant pants). Openings are sometimes 'sailor style' with a front flap and rows of buttons—with lacing in the small of the back. Cuffs optional, but these can shorten the legs if you're not tall.

KNICKERBOCKERS—originally worn by golf-playing chaps, they're essentially trousers that have been cut off below the knees and gathered (or pleated) into cuffs secured with a button or buckle. A masculine style that looks good on women. The best versions are tweeds for old-school style or polished cotton for New Romantic 1980s revivals.

SUIT TROUSERS—based on men's styles with centre-front fly and waistband with belt loops. Although often worn as a separate, these trousers generally come with a matching jacket and are favourites in the corporate world. Suit trousers are rather prone to the vagaries of fashion trends and recent years have seen the waistband sink down to the hips and then back up to the waist.

PEDAL PUSHERS—forever associated with 1950s soda fountains, a cross between a capri and a knickerbocker—fitted, but with the cuff-less hem finishing a little below the knee, perhaps with a small vent. These look great with ballet flats, a vanilla malt and a young James Dean wannabe.

"Service" Slacks
in fine wool jersey

26P3—Perfectly tailored Slacks with flat zippered placket and stitched creases down front of leg. Navy, grey or brown. 24 to 32in. waist. Price **18/11**

At left

Fine striped wool worsted

"Calamanco"
SLACK SUIT

In firmly woven worsted with slimming and very smart double stripe. Blue, aqua, wine or rose with white stripe.

26P4—The **Jacket Shirt** with two-way neck. Bust 32 to 38 ins., **29/11**

26P5—The **Slacks** are superbly cut with self belt and zipper at side. Waist 24 to 32 inches. Price **29/11**

A BRIEF HISTORY OF LADIES' TROUSERS

A highly politicised garment, trousers for women have slowly infiltrated our wardrobes since Turkish-style bloomers were introduced by radicals in 1849 as an alternative to the excessive skirts and petticoats of the time.

Trousers remained on the fringes of Western dress until the 1890s when they became the perfect garment for ladies who wished to ride bicycles and retain their modesty.

Fashion designer Paul Poiret took bloomers one step further in the early twentieth century by introducing Oriental-inspired 'harem pants', but the resistance to give up skirts was strong.

Beach and lounging pyjamas became popular among the leisured class in the 1920s and 1930s and were loose, flowing and elegant, worn with matching tops and jackets.

During World War II, the need for women to take over the roles that men had previously performed saw many wearing trousers and overalls—and off duty, high-waisted, flared shorts were worn for exercise and fun. After the war, women continued to find these styles useful for household chores and sports.

Trousers had found a permanent place in a lady's wardrobe, but it was a purely functional one—when it came to looking nice, she still reached for a dress or skirt. During the 1960s that changed, and, increasingly, jeans and pants were worn by the young and the radical who were forging a new fashion path.

Finally in the late 1960s, trousers became 'smart' and were worn as suits with matching jackets. That style went one further in the 1970s with men's style tailored waistcoats, often worn with feminine frilly blouses to soften them. It took disco in the late 1970s to introduce trousers to evening wear with sexy jersey versions.

The consternation caused by women adopting a traditionally male garment illustrates the political power of dress. By simply wearing an item allocated to the opposite gender, women were seen to be engaging in an act of rebellion and revolution. For most it was simply about having the freedom to wear whatever they wanted.

SHORTS

The fun little sister of the trouser, shorts are great for a hot day, especially if you're going hiking or cavorting.

SHORTS STYLES

BIKE SHORTS—nice, stretchy shorts introduced in the 1950s specifically for cycling, they also make a good multi-function garment to wear under very short dresses.

FLARED—short versions of flared trousers, these are more modest and pleasingly girly in style. They come in a variety of lengths and are sometimes full enough to resemble skirts.

SHORT SHORTS AND HOT PANTS—the tiniest of shorts, cut high on the leg, popular in the early 1970s when they were sometimes worn under open-fronted maxi skirts.

MADRAS OR BOMBAY BLOOMERS—man-style loose shorts that fall almost to the knees. Usually made in thick cotton drill and good for jungle treks in tropical locations.

WAISTCOATS AND VESTS

Waistcoats are sleeveless styles based on the menswear item and come in a few varieties. They make a good addition to layered looks and are often worn for extra warmth.

WAISTCOAT AND VEST STYLES

WAISTCOATS—usually feature centre-front buttons, with or without a tie in the back for shape. Pockets (with or without flaps) are generally of the faux variety nowadays, but higher quality or vintage garments may have small pockets, intended for a fob watch or handkerchief. When buying, it pays to check whether pockets have been stitched shut, as was often done by tailors—a small opening at one end will be left to facilitate cutting the stiches.

VEST—a simplified waistcoat, although the words are often used interchangeably. A knitted vest looks like a sleeveless jumper, with a crew or V neckline.

GILET—a modern version of the waistcoat, generally plain in cut and produced in leather, fur (real or faux) or wool.

JACKETS

Jackets can be mini coats or tops with big ideas, and come in assorted lengths and styles. They are generally an over-garment with a front opening with or without fastenings. Sleeves are usually long, but occasionally fashion brings short and three-quarter sleeves (bracelet length).

Jackets are particularly useful for weather or temperature changes, and are more formal or structured than a cardigan.

There's a certain amount of overlap between some heavier jackets and lighter or shorter coats—and the jacket has to some extent replaced the traditional overcoat, especially when worn with a scarf for extra warmth in winter.

JACKET STYLES

CROPPED—above the waist, a style that is excellent for highlighting a small waist or balancing out large hips, especially if loose or boxy in style.

BOLERO—a cropped jacket with an open front.

SWING—the body flows from the shoulders with a wider girth at the hem than the waist or hips, similar to an A-line or flare. A flattering style for ladies with curvy hips.

FITTED—tailored into the body with a defined waist shape: best for hourglass figures.

BLAZER OR BOXY—straight down from the bust to the hem, with no defined shaping. A great style for ladies with thicker waists and slim hips.

CARDIGAN—a soft style popularised by Chanel and now much copied.

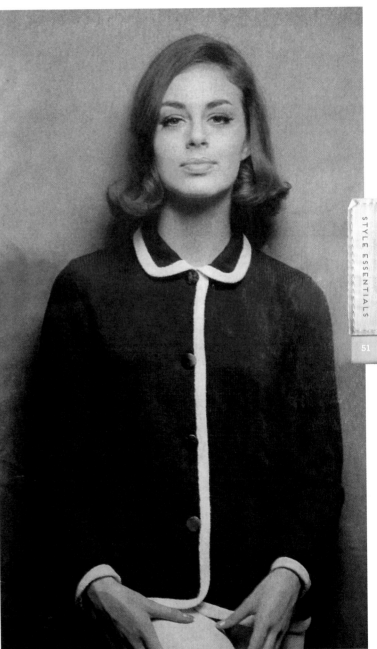

CHOOSING A JACKET TO SUIT YOU

It is vital that any jacket fit you perfectly, with tweaking if necessary, and the most important thing is the cut of the shoulders. They should sit comfortably and fall neither too wide nor too short of your own. Do up the jacket fastenings and move your arms gently backwards and forwards: the jacket should move with you and not needlessly constrain you. If the shoulders feel uncomfortable or do not sit well, seek a different size.

Next, look to the sleeve length. The cuff should sit level with your wrist bone when your arms hang relaxed, allowing a suitable amount of shirt cuff to peep through. Too long and you'll look like you're dressing in mum's clothes, too short and you'll look like a teenager after a growth spurt. Length can usually be altered, and by feeling along the cuff you can determine how much fabric has been folded back, indicating how much they can be taken down if they are too short. Long sleeves can always be taken up. Modern fashions are designed for ladies of 175cm so taller ladies may find sleeves too short.

Your waist is the next important part—the jacket should sit in the right place. Too high or low and the whole look is thrown out, unless it can pass as a design element. Your waist is the slimmest part of your torso, and is generally about 20 centimetres above the widest part of your hips. If the jacket waist is not in the correct place you may be able to alter it, but generally I would recommend choosing another garment, as a misplaced waist will not flatter your figure.

Many styles of jacket are not fitted at the waist, so they're great for ladies who prefer not to highlight this part of their body. Look for swing or boxy jackets especially.

If the jacket is a fitted style, it's recommended that you move in it, walk a little and perhaps sit down, to determine how comfortable the fit is. Consider the armholes and whether they are too high: can you move your arms in full range or are you restricted? (Windmills are not necessary, unless you do them regularly!) If it's not a comfortable jacket, you won't wear it and the purchase will have failed.

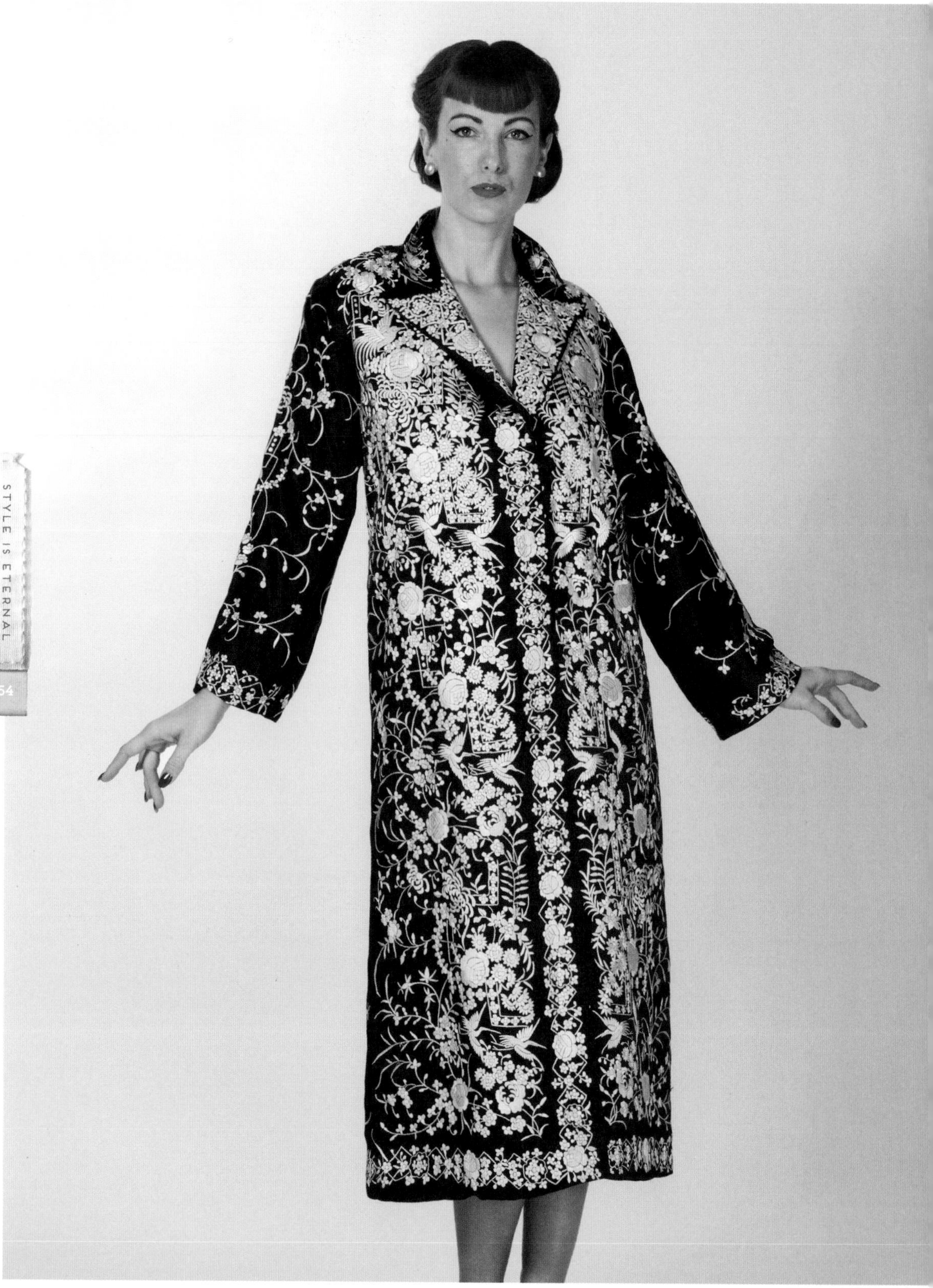

COATS

Coats follow similar silhouettes to dresses and jackets, with the two main shapes being 'fit and flare'—defined by a narrowing from the bust to the waist flaring out into an A-line or full skirt—or loose and boxy, usually quite straight with little variation in width. Trench coats fall into this category. A third option is the swing or trapeze coat, which flares out from the shoulders to a wide hem. This style is most flattering when worn shorter, mid-calf or above, due to the mass of fabric in longer cuts. Lighter fabrics will have more 'swing'.

If you like to wear skirts and dresses of a particular length, consider the same length for your coat, as it will suit them well.

Ideally, jackets and coats should be fully lined, preferably in a coloured silk, but many modern versions, especially in warmer climes, do not include this detail. Structured styles feature shoulder pads, as a strong shoulder line is flattering and balances out bust and hip curves. Softer and less formal styles might offer rounded or dropped shoulder lines without the padding.

Loose coats should have pockets, but fitted styles should either have faux pockets or none at all—if functional pockets have been included it's best not to over-fill them, as bulk can be unflattering. That is what bags are for.

The best coats will be constructed of fine wools, mohair, camel hair and cashmere. The latter is particularly desirable due to the softness and lightness of the fibre and is highly recommended for travelling or times when you will be out and about in a cold environment. An additional bonus is the quality of the material, which is sure to impress those who recognise it.

Protect your cashmere and quality wools, keeping them away from clothes moths, who will seek them out—dry clean all your coats and jackets at the end of the season and store them away from damp, insects and direct sun. Somewhere breathable—not in plastic, as it restricts the fabric—like a cupboard, wardrobe or cardboard box. If you choose a wooden receptacle, put a protective layer of fabric or paper between it and your clothes, or the oils might stain them: acid-free tissue paper is best, and available at art supply shops.

One effective protection is to roll up your garments in a cotton pillowcase, as the little critters will not show sufficient enthusiasm to eat their way through such a lesser-quality textile to reach their prize.

1.3
From
26/11

CAPES AND PONCHOS

An alternative to a coat or jacket is a cape or its groovier sister, the poncho.

Capes are generally fashioned from a circle or partial circle, perhaps attached to a collar and fastened with ties, hooks or buttons. They cover but do not restrict the arms, allowing freedom of movement. Sometimes they feature arm openings, especially in longer styles. They look nice lined with an attractively contrasting silk or acetate.

Ponchos are either circular or diamond shaped and symmetrical at the front and back, with an opening for the head only. They sometimes feature ties with pom poms as a decorative feature. Made of various materials, including knitted wool, they're often colourful and shorter than capes.

KNITWEAR

There are several different types of knits, producing different textures and patterns, but they all share one important characteristic: the material produced is endowed with a flexibility that will fit over any figure, as long as sufficient material is available. Knitwear isn't bound by the usual rules of warp and weft threads, where a garment will not sit well if it isn't cut along the right grain; this is why knitted garments require minimal seams—in fact some have none at all.

An added bonus is that, with the exception of fine knits, they need less washing and ironing, and so they make excellent travelling companions.

Although we associate jumpers and cardigans with knitwear the most, the technique can also be used to great effect in dresses, pants, tops and coats. Ponchos are another good use of knits, as are gloves, scarves and hats. Our grandmothers could knit entire wardrobes including underwear, socks and hosiery!

Knits are easy to repair, with small stitches in matching wool. Knitting clothing and accessories is an enjoyable practice that can be combined with other activities that keep the hands free, although the cost of wool can be punishing.

There can be a lot of skill and work in a hand-knitted garment, and, sadly, it isn't always appreciated by its recipient. Hand-made knits in excellent condition are therefore common in the second-hand market, where they are often bargain priced: attention vintage shoppers.

In the fashion world, commercially made knits are common and available in a wide range of colours and make good basics for your wardrobe, especially in winter, but cotton and silk knits are lovely items to wear in summer too. Note that cotton knits do not hold their shape as well as other materials, so look for a small synthetic component.

ACCESSORIES

Accessories are your friend. They are an invaluable part of your style and can be a lot cheaper than clothing. They're not affected by changes in body shape (with the possible exception of shoes) and are an easy way to update your wardrobe.

Accessories can also transform an outfit from day to evening or from one season to another. The right accessories can expand your wardrobe a great deal without using much extra space or cash.

SHOES

Where would we be without shoes? You probably have several pairs. You might even find that they breed when you're not looking, or perhaps they're irresistible things of beauty to collect.

MUST-HAVE SHOES

- ☒ a pair to wear to work (including if your work is at home)
- ☒ a pair to wear for dressy occasions (if you don't own these, you should)
- ☒ a pair to wear for relaxing
- ☒ a pair for exercise
- ☒ a pair you can wear on the beach or on hot days

You might find that you can combine some of these categories, but you will need at least two pairs—for hygiene's sake as much as to mix it up. Having only one style limits your sartorial choices too. If you find a pair you really love, think about buying two of the same style, perhaps in different colours.

Your work shoes should suit the purpose of the occasion and common sense should always prevail. A work day spent on your feet will require practicality, perhaps endurance and, if your role is customer service, a level of attractiveness.

All work shoes, regardless of your role, can—and should ideally—be appealing. Is there any point in wearing shoes that don't make you feel your best? No other item of clothing will affect how you feel more than your footwear, and how you feel is reflected in how others perceive you. It's very hard to look glamorous when all you can think about is how much you'd like to take your shoes off.

In one of my first jobs, I worked in a cafeteria where covered shoes were required. At the time, very high heels were filling the shops and sensible old lady styles were more or less the only alternative.

SPRING,
SUMMER
1949-50

Twenty-ones

styled for graceful walking.

A solution was found with a nice pair of lace-up shoes with a low heel that offered protection as well as style.

Shoes dictate the outfit, and I always dress from the shoes up because I work on my feet on a shop floor and comfort is a priority. I believe that you should never wear anything you can't walk a kilometre in—but if few walking steps are needed, gorgeous but impractical shoes may be an option.

Shoe fashions change frequently. We've recently had a cycle of very high heels followed (as always) by a cycle of very low heels, before heel heights moved back into the middle ground that suits most people.

When fashion takes an extreme turn, there is generally an opposite style available for those who prefer it. If you can't see anything you like, wait a little and fashion is sure to offer you something suitable. Another option is to consider the back catalogue: in the world of recycled and vintage fashion there are no limitations, as long as the footwear you acquire is in good condition. Heels and soles are easily repaired and replaced, but avoid well-worn shoes, no matter how pretty, because they will retain the imprint of the previous wearer's foot, which is never comfortable. If you do choose second-hand shoes, make sure they're clean and deodorised before wearing.

Consider other needs you might have—enjoyment, for example. Many of us love and appreciate beautiful shoes, almost as artworks, and there's no reason why you should be constrained by practicality when it comes to such devotion. Everyone needs a hobby.

Vegans will prefer non-leather shoes and a variety of nice styles are available, but quality varies a great deal. I recommend using inner-sole inserts to help absorb moisture if wearing synthetic shoes.

More than with any other aspect of your wardrobe, take care to maintain the condition of your shoes, as small, easy-to-fix problems can quickly lead to major ones. Looking after your shoes will ensure they look after you.

HANDBAGS

In recent times we've seen the handbag return as the accessory *du jour*.

But not so very long ago a woman would have had many handbags to suit her needs. Large ones for every day use, baskets or string bags for shopping, small and elegant confections for evening occasions. She might change her bag every day to match her outfit, and, pre-1970s, she would probably have coordinated it with her gloves and shoes, maybe her hat too.

Women have always needed small receptacles for their belongings—prior to the modern period, these might have taken the form of hidden pockets inside skirts or small cloth bags secreted in the folds. In the 1950s and 1960s handbags took on a life of their own and were even made in matching fabric to go with a special dress or pair of shoes. Before the 1960s handbags were much smaller than they are today, and ladies carried only the essentials—handkerchief, lipstick and make-up compact, maybe a pen or pencil, or personal calling cards and a small amount of money in a purse.

Nowadays most ladies will have only one bag to carry them from day to night and maybe just one other small, fancy evening bag for special occasions.

Day handbags have grown to be the biggest in history— large, slouchy shapes came into vogue in the early 2000s, reinvented from the 1970s on an enormous scale. Whenever a vintage style returns it is invariably with a modern twist or worn in a different way—so whereas a 1970s secretary would have had trouble fitting her diary into her well-buckled shoulder bag, the modern equivalents can hide a small child or puppy easily.

MY HANDBAG MUST ...

☒ be large enough to fit my diary, iPad or laptop, but no larger (carrying more than you need can result in injury)

☒ be easy to carry, even run with for when the bus comes early or you're running late

☒ look smart enough to be professional and relaxed enough to be used every day

☒ be different to my previous bag, otherwise, why change?

Larger handbags come at a price—the temptation to fill them is irresistible. Despite your best intentions, things that go in might get lost and forgotten in their crevices. A good supply of interior pockets, or perhaps a smaller bag within the bag, is helpful for access to items that might be needed in a hurry.

The counterpoint to a large day bag is a small and delicate evening bag. Though there is always the issue of where to put them—on the table, in your lap, on the floor where they could be easily dirtied or stolen? In the 1950s and 1960s, ladies could carry a small hook to use to hang their bag under a table, but these days no such option is provided. Styles with purse feet on the bottom are great for floors or a table, as they protect your bag and stop it from falling over.

Due to the important function handbags play in your day-to-day life, the purchase of a handbag warrants more consideration than almost any other item. From carrying your every need, to proclaiming your place in the world and complementing your wardrobe, it must be versatile above all else.

When choosing a new bag, consider your requirements: what it must contain, how you would like to carry it (in your hand, over your arm or shoulder, across your body) and how accessible its contents need to be.

My appetite for new handbags is voracious and I'm always on the lookout for a new, better style. When I recently broke my arm it was the first thing I changed, as I switched from a large, shiny, black, 1960s overnight bag resplendent with silver zippers to a small, red, 1970s shoulder bag with a strap long enough to sling across my body, enabling hands-free carrying. As my arm healed, I upsized again to a black DKNY with a textured leather finish to carry my laptop and more.

STATEMENT HANDBAGS

The trend of the statement handbag is all about something pretty to put on your arm that declares your style credentials (and income status) to the world. As well as being a beacon for thieves, sporting one of these bags will ensure retail staff follow you around their shop, as you are clearly not averse to splashing out.

Unfortunately handbags aren't the ideal investor piece—while care is always recommended, most will deteriorate with use and reduce their value. Perhaps due to the high cost of the most desired styles (and their long waiting lists), some will come onto the second-hand market long before the gloss on their appeal has faded—if you would like to save some money for other aspects of your wardrobe, investigate designer fashion auctions both locally and online, or designer recycled shops. Another option is to hire the preferred style from a specialist supplier and exchange it when you tire of it.

The prize of entering the pre-loved market has an added benefit of a potentially impressive provenance and if you look after your treasure, you can then on-sell when you wish. Certain designers and styles are particularly collectable—for example, original 1950s Hermès Kelly bags and Fendi baguettes. Scouring auction sites and specialist catalogues is your best bet for determining value.

Authenticity is key—designer fakes have been around for a long time, but became especially prolific in the last twenty years. Few design houses will authenticate items for you, so you might have to depend on either your own knowledge or trust the source.

Do not assume that second-hand items sourced from rich homes are necessarily authentic—many designer-label lovers will mix their collections with fakes (knowingly or unknowingly) and the only guarantee you have is an original receipt. Even then, be cautious! Professional appraisers can help and most auctioneers can recommend a good one.

SCARVES

Scarves come in all sorts of shapes, but the most common are square and rectangular. Designed to be worn around your neck, there are many different ways to wear them. Fold them in half, roll them up or twist them; knot to one side of your neck, down your back or front; tie them in a Windsor knot or fold them like a men's style cravat. Drape them loosely for a certain *je ne sais quoi*—glamour is always best when comfort meets charm. Scarves are the easiest of accessories as you can always pop them in your bag.

Scarves can also be worn around your wrist, around your handbag or your hair and, if long enough, around your waist as a sash or belt. Plait, knot, twist or thread them through a small buckle for an extra touch or secure with a scarf pin. Larger scarves can turn into stoles, worn over your shoulders. Pashminas, luxury versions in fine cashmere, are a convenient alternative to jackets and effective for keeping warm. The longer they are, the more versatile, but your scarf should never overwhelm you.

Do choose a complementary or contrasting colour—if you're wearing a print, work with the colours to introduce another print, a method that is popular in layering Japanese kimonos and obis.

Most scarves come in man-made fabrics like acetates or polyesters but silks feel nicer against your skin and impart a sense of luxury. For winter, fine wools and cashmeres will complement your coats and jackets.

Another option is to look to menswear: men's scarves come in classic colours like bottle green and burgundy, feature fringing or are reversible. They're often better quality for less money too. A nice option is a 1920s silk knit opera scarf—soak it in an oxygen bleach to freshen up the cream colour.

The quality of the scarf is dependent on the quality of its fabric—the finest are silk twills, preferred by the doyen of the luxury scarf market, Hermès. Look for hand-rolled hems, and your investment will increase. Nice examples can be found for good prices in the second-hand market.

Printed silk scarves should generally be dry cleaned as the colours can run—if laundering is necessary due to marks or dust, wash in lukewarm water with a mild detergent, rinse until the scarf relinquishes its suds, and gently squeeze out the excess water. Dry flat on a towel in the shade to preserve the dyes.

I once panicked when I found a beautiful silk Hermès in my washing tub—I hand wash all my scarves—but with gentle treatment it survived its ordeal and seemed to be improved by it. Laundering does a great deal more to freshen an item than dry cleaning ever can and there's nothing as good as the smell of fabric that has spent a little time in fresh air. But please, take care.

HATS AND CAPS

There are two types of headwear—those worn for protection and those worn for decorative purposes. The basic styles combine both.

Hats worn for protection are usually related to the weather or for occupational hazards—a sun hat keeps you cool and shaded in summer and a winter hat might protect you from rain or cold.

The harsh Australian sun is the reason why our skin ages more quickly than that of our cousins in colder climes—while sunscreen is a must, a wide-brimmed hat is an easy and effective way to delay wrinkles on your face and neck. Chosen well, a hat can be a stylish addition to your summer wardrobe, especially on the beach when clothing is at a minimum.

Back in 1970s Australia, we enjoyed a sun-worshipping culture oblivious to the consequences—so, looking at the people around me, I thought it was normal that at thirty my face would show many lines. Only when I lived in the UK did I realise what a difference that sun exposure can make. While it's hard to avoid the sun completely, it makes sense to take care. Once your skin is damaged, there is no repairing it, and it will forever make you appear older than you are.

We're fortunate that we don't experience very cold winters in the Southern Hemisphere, but felt and fabric caps and berets are a good way to keep your head warm and protected from the wind—plus, they can be folded up and put away easily.

A structured hat is a little harder to manage but packs a lot more stylistic oomph. Brims are generally smaller than those of sun hats. Preserve its shape by storing somewhere away from sun, dust and insects (a cardboard hat box or cupboard will do) and if the crown is likely to dent, pack acid-free tissue paper into it. Steaming with a steamer—or a boiling kettle— you can reshape any dents gently with your fingers: please be careful to avoid burning yourself.

For many of us, hats are associated with formal, daytime occasions like weddings, church and the races. Formal hats should coordinate with your outfit and for day events, softer feminine pastels and lolly colours are best—pinks, oranges, lemons and aquas—as opposed to darker, evening colours.

For a classic, foolproof, racewear look choose a black and white ensemble: dress and jacket with matching accessories including coordinated hat. Your outfit will dictate the correct headwear; large brims are best suited for simple ensembles as they add elegance—they can create too much noise with a busy outfit. Fascinators can provide an easy entry point for the unambitious but never impress as much as a proper hat, which is an opportunity to display the art of millinery.

Avoid wearing a hat that is so large it impedes your vision or movement. Make sure that it's quite secure on your head too. Some options to ensure this are the insertion of small hair combs; thin millinery elastic to sit around the back of your hair if worn long and down (choose the shade closest to your hair); or small loops of elastic (into which bobby pins are placed)—each of these are easily sewn into the inside band and invisible when worn cleverly. Good hats usually include the means of attachment, and a milliner—or hat department assistant—can advise you on how to best wear the style. Like all of your fashion, experiment with different ways to find which you like best.

Smaller women should keep to smaller hats as the large ones can engulf them, while the amazons among us can pull off much wider brims.

The label goes at the centre back, but you can wear a symmetrical hat any way you like. In the absence of a label, look for where the interior grosgrain ribbon joins: that should be the centre back. The hat should feel most comfortable when it's worn the correct way.

Your hairstyle will also dictate the best hat—cloches and small helmet styles are great for ladies with short hair, especially bobbed, while long hair, worn up (or down), will suit brims. Some faces look best with upturned brims and some with down—try on a variety of styles to see which works best for you. It's also worth considering a hat in a contrasting shade to your hair colour—white hats are stunning on raven hair, and black looks good on blondes. The contrast can also be introduced with the addition of an ornament: hat pin, brooch, rose or feather.

If you change your hairstyle or hair colour, seize the opportunity to add variety to your hat collection.

It should go without saying that a hat should be worn in the season it was designed for, or you are likely to look like you just got off the plane from another country.

For a form of hair adornment appropriate to an indoor evening event, for example a ball or party, consider a fancy hair comb or clip. Here is an occasion at last where fascinators can be appropriate, if not too large or ostentatious. Secure firmly if you intend dancing in it, or you might see it flying across the room.

GLOVES

The easiest way to add glamour to an outfit is to wear gloves—these come in several lengths, differing according to occasion, time of day and the outfit they're being worn with.

The big department stores should have a good range and you can always find interesting styles in speciality shops.

Gloves are generally made of fine, knitted materials, to provide both excellent fit and a good range of movement. In previous eras they were made of cotton, silk or wool, but the twentieth century saw an increasing use of rayons and nylons. Modern gloves are generally made of synthetic fibres (polyesters and Lycra) which lend them a certain shininess and resistance to dyeing. For the right colour you might have to search far and wide. First, try specialist retailers like vintage, burlesque and costume shops.

The longer antique and vintage gloves often feature wrist openings and small pearl buttons to facilitate dressing. In the 1920s ladies would undo the openings and put their hands through them to eat, without removing the whole glove. These days, most are very stretchy and so easy to put on and remove later. Volunteers to help remove them are generally easily found, and, if desired, this can be a great seduction tool!

Gloves can be hand washed and should be dried flat on a towel to avoid peg marks. Cotton and rayon versions can be soaked in oxygen bleach to remove marks.

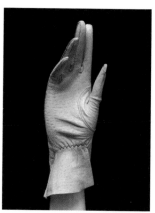

If you live somewhere cold enough to wear gloves in winter, lucky you! Lovely, soft, leather versions are available in a range of styles and elegant winter colours, either pull-on or securing at the wrist with a clip or button. Sizes correlate to your shoe size. Why not select a colour and style that goes with your favourite coat, so you always feel put together? Or match to your car, Tamara de Lempicka style—yellow and black were her favourite.

Nice linings can enhance your enjoyment for not much extra cost—I was delighted with my silk-lined, soft, Italian leather gloves until I discovered that the cashmere lining is even nicer.

GLOVES FOR ALL OCCASIONS

WRIST LENGTH—the shortest of gloves, perfect for a day event like a wedding, the races or afternoon tea. Colours are light (think cream, white and pastels) or lace or netting. Crocheted versions have the advantage of being stretchy, to fit most hand sizes. Best worn with long, three-quarter or short sleeves.

BRACELET LENGTH—above the wrist but below the elbow, these are an elegant length designed to show off your arm jewellery and look great with half sleeves or short-sleeved dresses. Can be plain or ruched along the sides with elastic. Good for dressy day events (light colours) or in dark colours for elegant cocktail parties. Fancy versions look best teamed with a plain dress, and vice versa.

ELBOW LENGTH—the all-purpose evening glove, for dressy night events. Will suit all events from parties, proms and cocktails to dinners and weddings. Nice in dark or bright colours to suit your dress, plus elegant when worn in lace. Gloves in this length can always be worn scrunched down a little with a longer sleeve, but they're best for short-sleeved or sleeveless dresses.

ABOVE THE ELBOW—this underutilised style is seen more in vintage gloves than modern ones and is best suited for a dressy, sleeveless, evening gown, cocktail or a very glamorous, full-length frock just short of a ballgown. As with all gloves, there should always be a decent amount of skin between where the glove finishes and the sleeve begins.

OPERA LENGTH—the very longest gloves, they climb to the top of your upper arm, where they complement the grandest of gowns—wear with your best strapless or strappy ballgown; the thinner the straps, the better (ballgowns with wide straps look best with an above-the-elbow glove).

FINGERLESS—these come in all lengths, in plain or fishnet, burlesque style. Any glove can be converted to fingerless if desired—depending on the fabric, you may wish to hem the cut-off fingers, but nylon and polyester knits don't fray much, and the raw edges can lend a certain character. These gloves downgrade the glamour by introducing elements of cabaret and connotations of poverty. They can be a good theatrical touch and also suit 1980s Madonna-revival looks.

Spring's on hand!

with gloves more feminine, more fashionable than ever!

We're pleased as Punch with our new Spring-Summer Collection, and we think you will be, too —includes every fashionable length from shorties to 8-button elegants. If what you want is not here, then do write—we're sure to have the gloves you want in stock!

A-44Q-241: ¾ NYLON SIMPLEX SLIP-ON. Smartly shirred style — quick-drying, of course, and miracle value at the price. White or Bone colours. 6½, 7 and 7½. 4 ounces. Pair, 14/11

B-44Q-242: EMBROIDERED NYLON SIMPLEX by "Collins", new season colours, including White, Bone and Devon. Please send sample when sending for colours. 6½, 7, 7½. 4 ozs. Price, 16/11

C-44Q-243: KAYSER NYLON STRETCH — imported fabric, quick-drying, a s-t-r-e-t-c-h glove to fit any hand. You'll love the firm cuff band! Bone and White. Weight is 4 ounces. At 9/11

D-44Q-244: "CRISTALLON" NYLON SIMPLEX, imported from Germany — will wear well, look marvellous! Neatly fitted cuff. Bone, White, Black. 6½, 7, 7½. Weight 4 ounces. Pair, 15/11

E-44Q-245: IMPORTED NYLON SIMPLEX SHORTIE with new, smart "Cristallon" finish that launders so beautifully. Snug mock cuff; in White, Bone, Red. Sizes 6½, 7 and 7½. 4 ounces. 12/6

F-44Q-246: ITALIAN DOUBLE WOVEN NYLON SIMPLEX, tailored style, goes with everything, wears wonderfully. Beige, White and Lemon. 6½, 7, 7½ sizes. Weight 4 ounces. Pair, 10/11

G-44Q-247: ¾ IMPORTED GLOVES—Dainty embroidery forms soft shirring on arm. With "Cristallon" special-launder finish, too! In White, Black, Bone. Sizes 6½, 7, 7½. 4 ozs. Pair, 19/11

Please add postage — see page 74

HORDERNS' CATALOGUE 1960-61 PAGE 19

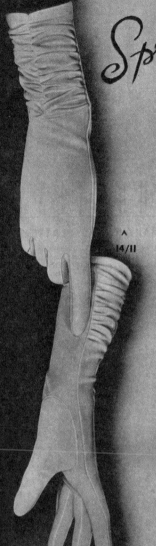

A
14/11

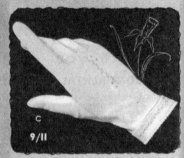

B
16/11

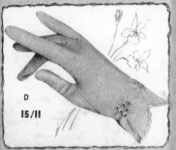

C
9/11

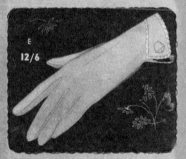

D
15/11

E
12/6

G
19/11

F
10/11

STYLE ESSENTIALS

81

Golden Age

K012
11/6

Top: Sheer
K012 — High-grade pure-silk Hose, "Golden Age" Service Sheer. Snug fit and smooth appearance. All new shades, 11/6

Hose Above
K013—Chiffon pure-silk Hose with dainty picot tops. The exquisite clear texture will delight her, Price... 9/11

HOSIERY

As with other elements of fashion, hosiery is worn for practicality, attractiveness or both. It's an under-appreciated way to add a colourful element to an outfit, especially in winter when we tend to favour dark colours. They look particularly sharp with boots and are easy to store and travel with.

Modern hosiery is generally made of synthetic fibres (polyesters and their stretchy cousins, Lycra and spandex), and comes in a range of weights or thicknesses called deniers, a word which describes the number of needles used to manufacture the product: the more deniers, the thicker (or more opaque) the hosiery, hence fifteen denier will produce a sheer product, and sixty will be better for winter warmth.

Hosiery has a fine history that goes back to the Middle Ages when it was worn by men as 'hose'. Ladies have long worn them under their dresses for warmth, held up by garters, and they became increasingly decorative during the nineteenth century when a view of a nicely turned ankle was highly prized. Patterns, called 'clocks', were woven in or embroidered, and many lovely examples can be found in museums.

Until the 1920s, all hosiery was made of natural fibres: wool, silks and cottons—then rayon was introduced, but the lack of a fine weave made it less popular than sheer silks, worn with a stitched seam up the centre back. During World War II nylon became available, and this was the standard material used during the 1950s. The next innovation was the introduction of machines that could produce a stocking without a seam in the 1960s.

KNOW YOUR HOSIERY

STOCKINGS AND GARTER BELTS—available in a range of deniers, although colours are generally limited to nude and black shades. Also common in seamed and fishnet versions. The advantages of stockings are twofold: they're better for hygiene as they allow free air movement, and they're sexier than pantyhose. A nice bonus is that they can remain on when your knickers are removed—although garter belts are generally photographed over knickers, they're actually worn the other way around.

HOLD UPS OR STAY UPS—similar to stockings but with a wide band of elastic at the top, with no garter belt required. They come in similar ranges to stockings and similar price points. Lace tops are a particularly nice touch and brides are fond of white versions.

PANTYHOSE—one piece with an elasticised waistband. The vast majority of the hosiery market is taken up by pantyhose, which has the widest product range and lowest prices. The downside to pantyhose is that they can be unhygienic. If this is a concern, some styles come with cotton gussets, or the gusset can always be removed. Some pantyhose feature reinforced 'knickers' and toes/heels. Fully sheer feet are recommended if you're wearing open-toed shoes or sandals. While the name suggests that they incorporate underpants, wearing underwear underneath is best for comfort and hygiene.

SUSPENDER HOSE—these styles supply the benefits and aesthetic qualities of stockings in the easy-wear format of pantyhose. The product range is very limited.

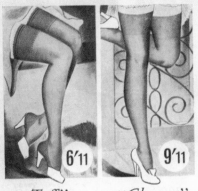

Buy "PRINCE CHARMING"
and learn what value in stockings really means!

"Tuff"
a three-thread crepe

17P9—Truly elegant Stockings of pure silk, beautifully knit and strengthened at all points of wear. In fashionable shades. Sizes 8½ to 10½. At **6/11**

"Charme"
a finely knit crepe

17P10—Delightfully fine and dull pure silk crepe Stockings, perfectly tailored and well reinforced. In all smart colours. Sizes 8½ to 10. At **9/11**

"No. 300"
fine mercerised lisle

17P13—Serviceweight lisle Stockings for day or sports wear. Dark fawn, burnt tan, grey or "curtsy," a neutral beige. 8½ to 10. Priced at **5/11**

"No. 400"
mercerised lisle sheer

17P14—Sleek fitting, sheer knit Stockings with comfy stretchy top. In dark fawn, burnt tan or "curtsy," a neutral beige tone. Sizes 8½ to 10. Priced at pair **5/11**

Polyesters were introduced in the 1960s, along with shorter skirts—with shorter skirts, there was more focus on the legs, and so a wider range of colours and patterns became available. With shorter skirts, came also embarrassment about revealing stocking tops and the thigh that appeared above them—and the enthusiastic response of male admirers. It was time to rediscover the neglected 'hose', and so pantyhose (a marrying of panty and hose) came back into vogue.

Stockings then began to be seen as an old-fashioned style, favoured by older women and those who didn't wear mini skirts. Then during the 1970s they were shunted into the shady domain of men's magazines and stag films, the preferred choice of mistresses and wanton women, eager for the pleasure of men. Respectable shops stopped carrying them, and the product choice was greatly reduced, while the range of pantyhose expanded.

These days you can get a fairly good range of both—especially in winter, when interesting colours, patterns and textures are available. In summer, you can find lace and variations on fishnets in a range of colours.

Both come in a range of sizes too, with taller also good for larger sizes (regardless of height). Size is less important for stockings, as the length of the garter belt strap can be adjusted, although some ladies prefer to wear them higher rather than lower for comfort's sake.

Stocking wearers should choose a garter belt that you're comfortable in—most styles on the market are 'boudoir' items that look nice but are not terribly practical. You'll soon discover their limitations after a day of wearing as they creep down your hips. I recommend wide garter belts with four straps (six if you wear seamed stockings, to keep them straight) and metal clasps—these will endure many washes. Some form of elastic fastener around the waist, generally where they fasten, will help them move with you, and stop them from falling down. Your garter belt should sit just below your waist—gently tug on the straps, and if it slips down, choose the next size down.

All hosiery should be hand washed (or washed in the machine in a special hosiery bag) as often as you wear it. Line dry rather than tumble dry, or hang up in your bathroom—they don't take long to dry, and, as long as you avoid snagging them, you should get many years' wear out of them. Some of my stockings I've had since the 1980s.

There's no reason to throw out your hosiery when they rip: apply a little clear nail polish to the torn threads and the run will go no further. If the hole is in a visible spot, save them to wear with boots or long skirts. More robust styles can be mended when ripped, especially lace, fishnets, wool, silk and cotton versions, but it is a rare lady who mends her hosiery these days, as inexpensive replacements can be found.

Laddered stockings at the end of their life can be recycled into hair bands and cleaning cloths—or cut out the crotches and feet and wear them as tops with the legs for sleeves. This easy, one-size-fits-all top is good for when you want coverage but not bulk.

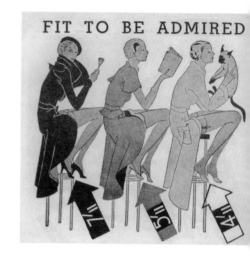

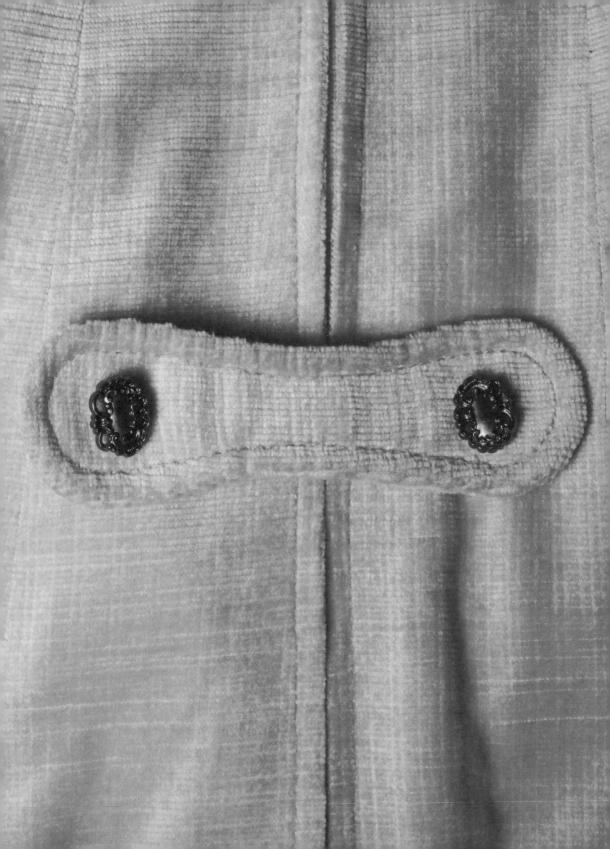

HOW TO DRESS

Pencil
Skirt

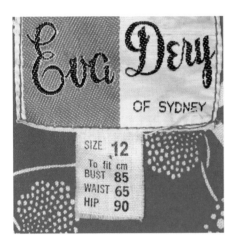

ere are some tactics to help you when putting a look, or a wardrobe, together.

DRESS FOR YOUR FIGURE TYPE

Like everybody, your shape will have its strengths and weaknesses, and it is unlikely current fashion will suit your particular set of idiosyncrasies season after season.

The great news is that almost without fail a fashion will have been done before—rather amusing when you consider that it's touted as the newest and freshest. The repetition gives us an opportunity to peek into the back catalogue if we don't like the current styles or want to foretell what might be coming up next.

Fashion of any era can be updated to look good now—the important thing is that you choose what will work for you, not necessarily what is currently in vogue. You'll probably find it easier than you think.

Every era of fashion focuses on certain parts of a woman's body. Find an era that is kind to your body shape and you will unearth a treasure trove of tried and tested ideas about how to make the most of it.

What do you like most about your figure? Do you have legs that stop traffic, a pert little bum, or shapely toned arms? Maybe it's your swan-like neck or voluptuous cleavage that garners the most compliments.

When you've found what you like most about your body, you can ask people you trust for a different perspective on your best assets too. Or, consider the parts of yourself you're not so keen on: the parts that you'd prefer to keep covered up, away from the gaze. For example, I'm shy about my feet— they're perfectly good feet, I just don't like to expose them.

FASHION FOR ALL SHAPES

Let's look at some different eras and how the fashions of the time can help you show off, or downplay, certain aspects of your body in your modern wardrobe.

1920s-style shifts and drop-waisted styles love slim hips and legs—and are great at disguising small breasts and thick waists. Not so good for ladies with curves, as they flatten them and can make you look frumpy.

1930s bias cuts and soft structures love shapely arms and a well-defined back—soft and slender curves are shown to their best advantage. A great decade for tall and athletic ladies too, but unflattering for the heavy-set among us.

1940s styles emphasised broad shoulders and a trim waist with tailored skirt suits and fitted dresses with A-line skirts—great for showing off shapely legs and hourglass figures, but ladies with less curvy shapes would do better to look elsewhere.

1950s silhouettes were all about womanly curves: the hourglass shape reigned supreme. Lovers of femininity will find a lot to love in styles of this decade. As well as emphasising curves with full skirts and nipped in waists, the shapes also provide curves to slim figures. Flat-chested dresses featured low backs to highlight another aspect of a woman's body.

1960s styles preferred a youthful, almost childlike silhouette with the emphasis on slim arms and long legs—great for ladies with minimal curves, nice legs or thickish waists. These simple styles do curvy figures no favours though.

1970s fashion emphasised nice legs and bums with skin-tight flares, mini skirts and knee-high boots. The more modest may choose flowing maxi skirts or *Little House on the Prairie* style fashion with wholesome, printed cottons, à la Laura Ashley.

1980s fashions became looser. Early in the decade, hip belts emphasised hips and bellies, and were perfect for hiding extra weight, while off-the-shoulder styles revealed shapely shoulders and drew attention away from busts. Later in the decade styles became more glamorous, with the focus moving to slim waists to counterpoint the ever-increasing shoulder dimensions.

Create great looks by mixing elements from different eras! With panache you can carry off any look.

FABRIC

Fabric is a useful indicator when selecting clothes: after all, a garment is only as good as the raw materials. It's easy to be seduced by a lovely style of garment, but if poor quality fabric has been used you won't look as good as you could.

Always consider the fabric before you buy—from how it looks on you to ease of care (machine washable or dry clean only?) to how long it will last before looking shabby.

The most pleasing fabrics to wear are natural fibres, which breathe, making them more comfortable, and are hard wearing, as well as nice to touch. The downside is that they tend to be more expensive, harder to find and, in the case of silks and cashmeres, require more care. Other natural fibres include cotton, linen, hemp, bamboo, leather, suede, fur and various types of wool.

A cheaper alternative is reconstituted cellulose fibres like rayon and viscose which are made from recycled natural materials like wood and cotton pulp. They aren't as strong as natural fibres but do share some other qualities like breathability.

Most clothing, however, is now made of synthetic fibres: nylons and polyesters. In the last sixty years there have been great advances in this area, and polyesters—an umbrella term for synthetic textiles (which are also marketed under trade-marked names like 'Lycra' and 'Elastane') can now closely replicate the look and feel of natural fibres.

Polyesters are chemical compounds of petroleum, so will not absorb or release sweat or humidity, making them less than ideal for sportswear (despite their popularity) and hot climates. They can also wear out quickly and produce pilling more than natural fibres. Acrylic polyester that imitates wool is particularly prone to this. Pilling is unsightly but can easily be removed by cutting off the small, fluffy balls with scissors or a special implement.

These days it's difficult to avoid synthetic fibres—their easy-care properties (wash and wear, drip dry, crease resistance) were gratefully received by harried 1950s housewives who no longer had to spend hours at the ironing board or hand washing delicates. We've become accustomed to spending less time caring for our wardrobe and it does indeed free us up for more enjoyable pursuits.

Modern synthetics have improved on the earlier versions, but they share the environmental cost; their fibres refuse to biodegrade, which is a little frightening considering how much we rely on synthetics. Most of it ends up as landfill—as a culture we need to explore recycling possibilities or alternative fabrics in the long term.

One advantage of the lack of biodegradability is that all those cute 1960s and 1970s colourful polyester frocks are still around (while their natural fabric cousins have mostly perished) and make great, fun additions to your wardrobe or for dress up parties.

COLOUR

Colour is an essential wardrobe tool that can move your outfit from day to night, or different season or mood.

Neutrals will likely make up the largest part of your wardrobe, and provide versatility.

Neutrals are colours that often appear in nature and do not draw attention to themselves. They play well together, although you might feel a little drab or invisible as they aren't attention grabbers. A solution to this is to add careful bursts of colour as accessories to brighten the outfit up.

I once dressed a large group of actors for a film scene set in an art gallery—the script called for everyone to wear shades of beige, but the result looked really blah. The solution was found by adding small touches of red in the form of jewellery, scarves, belts and gloves to each outfit, which lifted the look and provided personality to the characters.

There are two basic ways to use colour: similar shades or contrasting shades. The first is pleasing on the eye and easily achieved—shades of blue perhaps veering into a near colour like turquoise, teal or aqua.

Examples of contrasting shades are blue and orange, green and red, and yellow and purple, but clashing colour combinations can work well too, like yellow and pink.

Colour can also be divided into warm or cool shades—and colours mix well together if you select all cool, or all warm shades—for example, orange, pink and red; or yellow, sea green and blue.

Colour is an easy way to brighten an outfit or take it from day to night. Any two colours can be mixed, perhaps with the addition of a patterned accessory or interloper—I used to think that black and navy could not be mixed until I saw someone wear a navy top, with a cobalt belt and black skirt. The belt prevented the woman from looking as if she had dressed in the dark.

Wear colours that make you feel good and, if you can, buy complementary items (tops and bottoms, dresses and jackets or accessories) at the same time to save work later. Fashion houses design their garments and colour ranges to work well together each season, so it can be helpful to follow their colour codes.

Don't write off a colour because you don't like it: there's huge variation in tones, and while one shade of yellow may make you look sallow, another may help you glow. Keep an open mind and experiment—shops are playgrounds!

Many of us like to wear black, the greatest of non-colours, and while it can be the easiest choice, it is greatly improved by either wearing a variety of textures (for example, lace, velvet, sheer chiffon) to produce visual interest or small splashes of coloured accessories, especially near your face, can be flattering. For example, a coloured scarf, hat or jewellery.

PRINTS AND PLAINS

Printed or plain? Ever the big question. Plain fabrics are best for showing off the silhouette or sculptured shape of a garment in their simplicity and are popular for evening wear, corporate wear, basics and sportswear. They allow the focus to be on the wearer. The downside is that they show up any flaw, and can be harder to clean or repair.

Prints are best for day looks, and are great at hiding flaws: from mends to stains—depending on the pattern, you'll find the issues hard to see. I'm sure this is why they became so popular for everyday fashion: their practicality is hard to beat.

Prints make wonderful accompaniments to plains and are a great way to add different colours, especially in small doses: wear a plain scarf with a printed dress, or a printed top with a plain skirt.

Good mixing of patterns can be achieved by using a similar colour palette—choose two dominant colours to tie the elements together, or perhaps a unity in print; different colours of polka dots or checks work well, especially in similar tones.

A third option is to use similar prints in different sizes, e.g., two florals, one larger and one smaller.

POPULAR PRINTS

SPOTS—polka dots, hailstone and random spots

STRIPES—pinstripes, chalkstripe, mattress ticking

CHECKS—tartan, plaids, gingham, houndstooth, dogtooth, Prince of Wales check

FLORALS—small or large, dark floral, antique style or abstract

GEOMETRICS—waves, zigzags, chevrons, herringbone, Art Deco style

NOVELTY PRINTS—animals, unexpected items like aeroplanes or clowns

ANIMAL PRINTS—leopard, tiger, zebra, giraffe and cow

ABSTRACT PRINTS—splotches and scribbles, modern art style

LINGERIE

What you wear under your clothes has a great effect on how they look and how you feel. Traditionally called 'foundation' garments, lingerie are the first garments you put on when you get dressed and you may as well get the best from them.

Fit is of primary importance—knickers should be of sufficient size as ill-fitting knickers can ruin your day.

French knickers, a charming and loose style resembling shorts, provide a stylish and comfortable alternative to fitted knickers.

Choose natural fibres for your knickers to avoid health issues like Candida—always read the fabric composition label, as many cute styles are nylon or polyester which are the main culprits. Most knickers contain at least some synthetic, but avoid styles where it's the major component, especially if you'll be wearing them frequently.

They say that most of us are wearing the wrong sized bra. Take care to get your bras professionally fitted, especially during body changes. Avoid baggy styles, or too tight, or styles that ride up or show under your clothes.

Repair or throw out any lingerie that is shabby and worn: not only does it look terrible, but it can also depress you much more than shabby outer clothes.

Investing in good quality and luxurious lingerie will pay dividends in how you feel. Very few other people may see it, but this is part of the pleasure: like having a secret. It will also make you feel less concerned about getting hit by a bus (highly unlikely, but mum did warn you).

Full-skirted crinoline petticoats lend fullness to full skirts and dresses, providing extra swish and 1950s style silhouettes. Petticoats and camisoles might seem old fashioned, but they offer protection between you and your clothes—reducing the need to wash them as the lingerie absorbs oils from your body and will smooth out lumps and bumps in your figure. There's a good reason why grandma never left the house without hers. I always wear mine too.

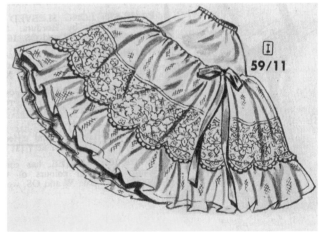

59/11

106

W308

W309

W310

B
19/6

C
27/6

E
25/-

G
69/11

24R6
$2⁷⁵

24R3
$1⁹⁹

DRESS WELL AT EVERY AGE

Once upon a time ladies would dress differently according to how old they were and where they were travelling in their personal life path—young women would wear their hair long and down, while older ladies wore it up. Young women wore bright colours and more flattering, revealing styles—while older ladies consigned themselves to other priorities.

Mostly this was a convenience for men, so they could easily identify the unmarried women, in the same way that a wedding ring signals unavailability: traditionally one for her, but none for him. Thankfully, these days we are no longer bound by old-fashioned ideas of dress. Men wear wedding rings too and women can dress to please themselves, no matter their age.

As a vintage fashion dealer, I'm well aware of the different functions originally assigned to dress types—and how the modern wearer doesn't feel constricted by them. Frou-frou prom dresses that were worn by teenagers in the 1950s are now sought after by ladies at all stages of their lives. You don't have to be an actual Prom Queen to dress like one.

The secret to looking good is wearing clothes that you feel good in, that express your personality and that fit you well—there's no reason why you shouldn't wear a particular style just because someone perceives you as being 'too young' or 'too old'. Trust your own opinion and give an ear to those you respect.

I used to have a neighbour in her seventies who rocked a disco wig and hotpants, her tanned and wizened face shaded in wrap-around sunglasses. She certainly had the legs for it. She was my hero—wearing so-called 'inappropriate' fashion when others were slipping quietly into nursing home comfort. Go disco lady!

The internet, courtesy of blogs like *Advanced Style*, highlights older people dressing stylishly. In general, older people know how to dress because they grew up in a time when you didn't leave the house without the right outfit—for ladies this included gloves and matching handbag. They had limited resources and knew how to put an outfit together and have had years to practise their skill. They know themselves and what works best for them and don't care for short-lived trends. There are lessons there for all of us.

Many style blogs by younger people trade on their slim figures and good looks—with a bit of attitude you can look good in almost anything. Youth is a great time to experiment, be brave and make mistakes, but the older we get, the more we have to make an effort, as our bodies change, our faces wrinkle and our hair greys.

We might find we need to wear glasses, when we previously had perfect vision. Or our shoulders might round forwards, as we lose muscle tone. We might put on, or lose weight, or it might be redistributed in pesky places.

If you do find your body shape has changed, look upon it positively as an opportunity to venture into a sector of the fashion world previously unknown to you. Let go of your perception of your body shape, and try on different styles. What worked before may not work as well, but new doors will open.

TIPS FOR ADJUSTING TO CHANGES

☒ If you find your body is now curvier, look to outlines with structure, for example a firm shoulder line balances a full bust, and resist the siren call of shapelessness.

☒ If you're now slimmer, ensure you're wearing the right size, as too big is unflattering.

☒ The length of a hem can make a lot of difference to whether your skirt looks chic or frumpy; find the right spot for you, and your preferred heel height.

☒ Thicker waists benefit from long line garments that skim your middle rather than hugging it—avoid tight clothes if your body is no longer trim and toned.

☒ Colour lifts ageing complexions, especially worn around the face in accessories or jewellery, and a lick of red lipstick can make teeth look whiter.

☒ If you no longer wish to bare your arms but still want to get use out of a sleeveless style, wear a top with more coverage underneath or a cardigan or jacket over the top. Sleeves can also be added to garments.

☒ Bold accessories like spectacle frames and jewellery are effective tools at drawing attention away from other aspects.

☒ Some people look fantastic with grey/white hair, but others find they prefer to dye. Colouring your hair offers you choices— do you go with the colour you were, or the colour you want to be? Embrace the freedom ageing brings; it is, after all, a privilege not everyone obtains, and it brings wisdom too.

☒ Don't be intimidated by others' ideas of what you should and shouldn't wear—wear your fashion with confidence and know that it's about what you want.

CREATING A LOOK

114

S tyle is about expressing who you are, or who you want to be, style is aspirational. It's about feeling good about yourself and feeling like 'you', happier and more complete.

Do you feel better when you wear roses in your hair? Why not wear them every day? What will happen? Probably, you'll get stared at in the street—by people who think you look lovely and by people who are thinking 'is that a flower in her hair? How odd.' Do you care about what those people think? It's impossible to please everyone, so isn't it more important to please yourself?

A rose in my hair once got me special treatment in a Sydney restaurant—for me it was an ordinary meal but afterwards, the waitress sidled up and whispered 'I could see you are special from the flower in your hair!' It made my night.

Style can make you stand out, sometimes uncomfortably so—especially for those of us who are introverts. Baby steps are called for: push the boundaries but no more than you're comfortable with. Start with a little bit of something out of the ordinary: an unusual colour or a small accessory that makes you smile. As you become comfortable and more confident, you can add more touches—a new jacket, higher heels, a fancy hat, and gloves to the opera. Accessories are a great way to experiment.

Never be afraid! Clothes can be changed out of immediately or at the end of the day. Other people, even if they look at you funny, can't really get upset. After all, they're just clothes.

Style can also be understated—the subtle look that doesn't scream 'look at me', but is pleasing to the eye. Style is always appropriate, even when it doesn't fit in with what your peers are wearing—never let your peer group dictate all that you wear, however much you wish to be like them.

The prize is a valuable one: personal creative expression. You are special and unique, and your life should be a celebration of that.

To figure out the essence of your style, ask yourself a few questions.

Who are you?

The answer to this question will be very complex, but let's just focus on the easy stuff. What do you look like? How old are you? Where do you live? What do you do for fun, for a living, in your downtime?

Think about yourself and your life—are you a waitress who needs to wear comfortable shoes and clothes that look nice and neat but are easy to wash spaghetti marinara out of? Are you a mum with a couple of small children who like to tug at your clothes? Are you a student on a budget who just wants to fit in? Your life makes physical and practical demands and your wardrobe should be built around these.

No matter your habits and no matter your budget, you can always inject personality and style into how you dress.

Who do you want to be?

This is a question about aspiration—where do you want to go? They say that you should dress for the job you want, rather than the one you already have, and it's true that in every occupation, your clothes can help you get where you want to go, whether it's fitting in with the boys in a blue-collar job or working your way up the corporate ladder. Your clothes can help you in many ways. They can also help you socially—what you wear will attract new friends as well as advertising to your existing buddies that you're one of them.

What suits you?

We all have colours that flatter us and those that diminish our charms—find the colours that appeal to you, and more importantly, look appealing on you, and seek them out. If you have limitations, for example, a job that requires you to wear all black, but black does you no favours, find other ways to enliven it, whether through accessories, make up or even colourful hair.

Some shapes will work better for your figure than others. I'm a firm believer that there is no perfect figure we should all aspire to, so we shouldn't waste any time beating ourselves up about what we have to work with, because even Kate Moss looks terrible in some things. As they said in the old song: 'You've got to accentuate the positive, eliminate the negative', and there is so much you can do with the right outfit. We all have strengths and weaknesses, and it makes sense to work to our strengths.

Of course, if you were suffering from adverse health effects because of the shape you're in, and you were working to improve these, I would encourage you—but in the meantime, fashion can help you look and feel fabulous.

Traditionally, Western fashion came from up on high: the kings and queens and their courtiers would adapt their dress to suit their purposes—it was status fashion, made of the richest of materials and ornamentation so that all who looked upon them could quickly determine the wearer's importance and respond accordingly.

New styles might have been chosen to highlight personal physical attributes, such as by Henry VIII, who liked to emphasise his solid stature through broad, puffed and slashed sleeves (revealing the rich linings within) and his masculinity with a large, padded codpiece.

His daughter, Elizabeth I, dressed in a warm colour palette of golds and reds, as they brought out the best in her pale skin and auburn hair—a palette that stamped itself on the era she reigned over, and tinges artworks of the time. Her sumptuous gowns were embellished with the fruits of her vast empire: gems, pearls and silk embroideries.

The courtiers would mimic the royal styles and they would in turn filter down to all levels of society, albeit in a very diluted form. For the very poorest, fashion changed slowly or not at all, as harsher realities demanded their scarce resources.

This division receded in the twentieth century, as marginalised groups of the working class, women and ethnic people fought to improve their lives and obtain greater rights in society. As each group has risen, the power of the ruling class to dictate tastes and values has diminished, and so has it been with the spread of fashion.

Fashion as we know it began in the Victorian era with the first great fashion designer, Charles Worth. The House of Worth and others, supported by the ruling class, became the originators of fashion, each season producing new styles that were generally released to great acclaim and which filtered slowly down.

The fashion silhouette during the nineteenth century to the 1960s changed roughly every decade, with minor decorative changes keeping things fresh for those who craved stimulation. Back then, you could get good value out of your wardrobe, which would have been important because clothes were expensive.

Where previously garments were handed down from the rich, bought on the second-hand market or sewn by the home seamstress, increasingly manufacture was commercialised—first after the invention of the sewing machine in the 1850s, then with industrialisation of clothing factories. After World War II came an enormous growth in the 'ready to wear' market, which produced affordable, everyday clothes for most people, while the home seamstress or professional dressmaker still constructed special-occasion wear. The upper classes wore couture—custom-made clothing of the highest quality.

Fashion was an adult concept—girls would look at their mothers, dressed in elaborate constructions of foundation wear, petticoats and gowns and yearn to be old enough to frock up so elaborately.

This system changed during the 1960s when two things happened: first, the 'baby boom' children, born after the soldiers returned home from World War II, were growing up and impatiently wanted their own fashion that spoke to their generation and was different to what their mothers and fathers wore.

Second, changes in trade rules opened up offshore manu-facturing in Asian countries where costs were lower, leading to reduced production costs. Fashion was still largely made locally, but this exerted pressure on the local companies to reduce their costs.

Reduced cost meant more fashion could be purchased, and the increased demand for new styles from young women created the modern trend of disposable fashion. Suddenly the fashion cycle sped up, and, instead of changing every decade, it seemed like every season offered something new and exciting.

Those who could sew were producing their own, home-made versions, and young designers were stepping up to offer popular styles with increasingly shorter hemlines—once, you had to have a solid backing to open a fashion label, but now teenagers like Prue Acton were setting up shop. The fashion cycle was now such that you could see a new dress style on TV and purchase it from a local boutique in a matter of days.

The implications were enormous: everyone wanted to be young, energetic and free. Even the elderly embraced the new, colourful and childish designs, baring their arms and legs in styles that were fun and playful. The old era of couture was over, and the power to set fashion trends now came from the street, from clothes that innovators wore, not the elite. This system endures today, and it's an egalitarian and democratic one—street styles that inspire are taken up by fashion houses and mass produced, and the more those sell, the more widely they will be copied and distributed for anyone to wear.

Here are some of the different ways you can express yourself: work with one of these, try a combination or find something entirely new.

ARTISTIC

Within every society there will be those who are creative and embrace the opportunity to express that creativity through their dress. They may do it cleanly in structured mono-chromes like architects and industrial designers, or they may be free spirits, playing with colour and texture like artists and textile designers.

These are the innovators, the people who help lead fashion into the next trend and see into the future. Watch them keenly for the insights they reveal.

Artistic people understand the full potential of fashion to tell a story or create a fantasy—like living sculptures—practical concerns are of less importance than making a statement or indulging their whims. They may dress in a particular way: always in a certain colour or textile—in black velvet or crimson silks, for example—or every day may suggest something new, like a character from a TV show, or another era.

As a child, I made dresses from broken umbrellas and torn sheets, which I hand-embroidered with stars—when you're very young you see no limits, but it's a credit to my parents that they were happy for me to go out in public in these potentially embarrassing ensembles. As I got older I found that the rules changed; our society is not so forgiving of those who dress outside of the square, and yet it holds up the greatest as icons.

Therefore the creative dressers among us must nurture either a thick hide, a disdain for the reactions of strangers and loved ones, or an eccentric personality to weather the unkind arrows that will come their way.

We need the non-conformers to inspire us and show us new and different ways of doing things. They embrace new technologies, colours and shapes, and were it not for these people, fashion would change slowly and timidly. The brave push boundaries and set trends, and we owe them credit for broadening our horizons and possibilities.

If you are among them, develop a strong sense of your own style outside current trends; consider unusual ways to wear orthodox garments and play with alterations or additions. Seek out forgotten fashions, long out of the limelight and ready for resurrection. In doing so, remember that every fashion style will soon produce its opposite, and the longer it has been away, the fresher and more appealing will be its return.

The bad girls of the 1950s wore their cardigans backwards and a size too small, inviting strangers to metaphorically unfasten the buttons, the waists nipped safely into wide leather belts and pencil skirts, in contravention of the prevailing full-skirted fashions.

When Alexander McQueen sent his models down the runway clad in enormous hoof-style boots we scoffed, but soon the style had been wrangled into a less challenging version and we were wearing skyscraper heels with obnoxiously chunky soles. Another season and they started to look completely chic. Fashion is an odd beast, forever craving the new and exciting.

Create the trend and you avoid becoming its victim.

CLASSIC

A perennial favourite for women of all ages but especially older ladies, 'classic' style is about dressing plainly with an emphasis on quality—the Chanel cardigan jacket is a perfect example of this: dressy enough to suit most occasions, but also sufficiently relaxed to be comfortable. Paired with a straight skirt it's a high-recognition piece that allows the quality of the workmanship and materials to shine through, but it also works dressed down with scruffy bleached jeans.

Classic style pieces are those that are most impervious to trends—well cut, and in proportion. They're resistant to exaggerations of the body, like extended shoulders, dropped waists or pointy busts. Year in and year out, your investment will pay dividends if you buy wisely.

They can make young women look older and older women look ageless, but need to be kept in good condition, or they can look sad and cheap. Classics are versatile though, and can work well mixed with trends to create a personal look. This avoids the staidness often called 'safe' dressing.

Classic style is also associated with a particular social status—set it off with prestige accessories and expensive jewellery—but can work for anyone, as long as one avoids too clichéd pieces and looks for simplicity. This look pairs well with 'elegance' and 'corporate' styles.

Lauren Hutton wears a classic style that is as popular today as it was in her heyday of the 1970s—wide-leg pants with waistcoats and loose man-style shirts in neutral colours. They suit her at every age due to her tall, slim figure and beautiful features.

CORPORATE

Many of us find the most demanding section of our closet to be workwear, and if you're employed in the corporate world that wardrobe can be a costly one.

The good news is that corporate wear is easy to understand, easy to obtain at all price points and easy to customise to your particular workplace or personal taste. It's also the most conservative of fashions, and slow to change, which means that ladies who bought up big in the 1990s are probably still wearing their suits to the office, albeit with a few modern touches.

Corporate wear as we know it originated in the 1940s when women stepped into all the roles previously performed by men, who had now gone off to war. Times were tough during World War II, and a suit was a big investment, so ladies bought the best they could afford: pure wool, naturally (there were no polyesters back then), fully lined in rayon twill with shoulder pads and functioning pockets, customised to fit perfectly. The matching skirt might have been A-line or straight depending on how many fabric ration cards she had.

The hourglass was the desired shape for a woman at the time, and a well-cut suit made the most of it. So she could wear it continuously, a plain and dark colour was usually chosen: black, grey, brown, burgundy, navy or bottle green—the colours, like the style, were borrowed from menswear.

Underneath she wore a thin blouse (perhaps so thin it was sheer) with a pretty frontage: the portion seen beneath the buttoned up jacket would reveal an attractive collar (shaped to suit the fashion of the day), or decorative buttons, lace or pintucking. When the budget did not allow, she might just wear a 'dickey', a fancy piece that would sit around her neck under the jacket.

Stockings were worn of course and sensible shoes that were pretty but also plain, with a mid-height heel so they didn't impede movement: after all, if the siren sounded she might need to run to the bomb shelter. Matching handbag and accessories completed the look. It was a serious style that projected professionalism while downplaying gender.

Since then, corporate wear has seen fewer changes than most styles of fashion—the classic 1940s look will still go down well in the modern office, especially if you go easy on the accessories and update your shoes. I speak from experience—my corporate wardrobe during my ten years in the IT industry included many 1940s suits and dresses, and the only comments they garnered were complimentary.

The suit is still the best base for a modern corporate wardrobe, and it's recommended that you have at least two good jackets with matching skirts and trousers—many labels offer separates in the same fabric, allowing you to change your look quite a bit. The colours are best kept to the classic menswear palette to avoid attracting too much attention (less attention equals more versatility in dressing).

Suit jackets are a much-neglected aspect of ladies fashions, but they lend a smart aspect, as well as warmth, as you travel to work or for meetings—even if they're taken off inside the office. A good jacket will also look nice when worn open over a dress—boxy and blazer styles work best here.

A nice dress is an acceptable alternative to tailored separates, but it should be a variant of dressy daywear, with any aspects of cocktail or evening dresses to be avoided—satins, sequins and beads are generally out unless you work in the most creative of environments. Tight and revealing clothing should also be kept to after-five wear, as it can be distracting for co-workers and also impacts negatively on perceived professionalism.

Good basics for the office are an investment but can be found at reasonable prices on the second-hand market, at charity shops and designer recycled shops, as well as online (although there's no substitute for trying something on).

Once you've found your day-to-day look, you can enjoy adding personal touches through tops and accessories—ensure that all are in good condition, as shabby is never a good look for work.

To identify appropriate dress for your workplace, inspect your co-workers' dress and, especially, your boss. You will be judged for your dress at work regardless of the quality of your actual contribution, and it will impact on your success—your outfit shows that you fit in, are part of the work culture and gives the impression of competence, which is a good start. It's not particularly fair, but it's human nature; we subconsciously decode information about each other. It's important to make that work to your advantage.

Fine Tweed
If you prefer this shade, tear off sample and send it with your order.

NATURAL

The counterpoint to a glamour look is the 'natural'or 'normcore'—to look as if no effort at all has been made (which, paradoxically, can be highly involved).

The two looks—glamour and natural—are the two main pillars of modern fashion, and styles tend to cycle between them, as much as a trend for long skirts will be followed by one for short skirts, and low heels follow high.

Natural was spawned by sportswear but has developed considerably, not least in having relinquished any pretence of actual physical activity. There is no requirement to be in the vicinity of any sport, and it's not even clear if the look could withstand the pressures of exertion.

'Natural' style in fashion is one that does not distort or exaggerate the body in any way—so it tends to be a loose, casual style, without visible foundation garments. It emulates the clothing of small children in its perceived practicality and lack of womanly charms—the mainstay of your wardrobe will be cotton knits like t-shirts, tracksuits, loose tops and bottoms.

Knits will also be there in jumpers, cardigans, perhaps something hand-knitted—these are clothes built for comfort and lack of restriction. Shoes will tend to be flat and functional: Ugg boots, Birkenstocks, crocs and thongs/flip flops. The natural thumbs their nose at status and 'fashion'. It can almost be said to be an 'anti-fashion' look.

While this look is the easiest because the bar is so low—you can find all you need in an op shop or budget retailer—the challenge is to look good.

We all have a place in our lives for this style of dressing, even if it's only for when you're performing household chores or the gardening, or running an errand to the corner shop. An outfit that is low maintenance and practical—but if it's sloppy and unattractive, you'll feel that way too.

To create an effective 'natural' outfit, start with good quality basics—preferably natural fibres (cotton, wool, silk) in simple styles and a simple colour scheme. No more than three colours at once, and at least one should be a neutral—black, grey and white are the most versatile examples, but you might choose navy or beige—if all your pieces fit into this colour scheme they will automatically work well together without any effort.

Then ensure that all pieces fit you well and maintain their condition (by either repairing or replacing as needed). Your shoes are especially important—scruffiness here can bring down your whole outfit. It's very hard to look good when your Ugg boots are dirty and bedraggled.

You can add accessories, but keep them simple: low-key sunglasses, a knitted beanie, an uncomplicated necklace or matching plain-coloured scarf. You don't want to look as if any thought has gone into your outfit—this look is about being relaxed, not standing out.

You can avoid looking slobbish by incorporating slight elements of structure: a well-cut shoulder, sleeves that are no longer than they need to be. A fitted waist rather than an elasticised one.

Kate Moss, who dresses very stylishly for her day job, slums it at Glastonbury Festival in cut off jeans and loose tops, worn with practical Wellies for any potential mud. Kate is a whizz at dressing down—part of the reason her style endures after so many years at the top. She truly looks like she doesn't care for fashion, so much so we suspect it's true.

DRESS FOR THE MOMENT

I f in doubt—dress up! There are many advantages to dressing up: feeling better, looking better, to name just two. People will treat you better. It worked for our grandmothers and it works just as well today.

There are many occasions where dressing up will win you a big nod and even sometimes a prize or two—the races, weddings, opera, ballet and theatre. Dressing well at a cocktail party or restaurant will attract the best service. Dressing your best at work will increase your chances of promotion.

Dress appropriately for each occasion, but keep in mind that it's always better to be over-dressed, than under-dressed. Here are some different ways you can dress your best.

ELEGANCE

Elegance is always a good look, and you don't need an occasion to indulge in a little of this quality.

Elegance is the key for day events like weddings and the races: channel a bit of Jackie Kennedy's style in smart dress-and-jacket ensembles with coordinated accessories—match shoes with hats and handbags, or, for something different, your lipstick or eye shadow.

'Matchy matchy' works well, but it's best to understate it by using complementary colours, or pick just one colour to 'pop'. If you're walking on grass or standing on your feet for hours, leave the stilettos at home, and choose block heels, wedges or stylish flats to avoid feeling uncomfortable.

The art of recognising good design and appreciating quality—elegance is in how you put an ensemble together and wear it for the right occasion, resisting the urge to overdo it, and letting your quiet confidence speak for itself.

Elegance can be costly but doesn't need to be: it's an attitude, confidence and subtlety. Chic rather than loud, quiet rather than brash.

An icon of elegant style is Audrey Hepburn—early in her acting career, Audrey had the good fortune of being dressed by French fashion designer Hubert de Givenchy for the title role in the film *Sabrina* (1954). The fashions in this film were central in illustrating the transition of Sabrina's development from gauche chauffeur's daughter to sought-after companion, pursued by two handsome men.

Hepburn became Givenchy's muse and they worked together on many subsequent projects. Her slim, gamine looks provided a counterpoint to the curvaceous charms of classic 1950s stars like Marilyn Monroe and Sophia Loren and were perfectly suited for displaying the structural qualities of Givenchy's designs. But Audrey's real decade was the following one, as her girlishness fitted the aesthetic ideals of the 1960s, with the success of *Breakfast at Tiffany's* (1961), where she immortalised the little black dress—a long and very simple version, worn with pearls and long gloves, and her hair in a high bouffant. Elegance personified.

In 1964 she wore an Empire-line evening gown in *My Fair Lady*, which perfectly suited her figure, elongating her form. Cecil Beaton's award-winning costume designs saw her in combinations of black and white—an eternally chic combination—with her hair styled up, and wearing extravagant Edwardian era hats for the racing scenes.

The key to Audrey's style is an uncluttered one with good quality design. Her fine features and figure would be swamped by fashions that were large, loose or loud—her elegance is about accentuating the charms, not hiding them.

Audrey was one of the few actresses who could believably play a princess as well as a beatnik. Elegance has a versatility that can carry you anywhere.

Coco Chanel would have approved of Audrey's style; in fact Audrey would have been the perfect model for the designer's fashions, were she not working with Givenchy. Chanel famously remarked that before leaving your home, you should look into the mirror and remove one item—but this was back in the days when accessories were king and ladies tended to wear lots of them. Perhaps nowadays she would be more inclined to remind us that we should put one more thing on? Accessories are an underappreciated part of the modern wardrobe.

Chanel, like Audrey, loved monochromes and wearing pearls that graduated from white to black with her little black

dresses and wool tweed suits. Perhaps the most successful of fashion designers, Chanel took inspiration from menswear and workwear and played a big part in the casualisation of twentieth-century womenswear—yet her name is now a byword for chic sophistication.

She encouraged women to leave their corsets at home, and dress simply in unstructured dresses of fabrics like jerseys, that previously were considered too déclassé for those with taste. She eschewed the fancy and overblown—and was ahead of her time. In many ways she liberated women from an old way of thinking and dressing. Her success was unprecedented—not only did she help shape the zeitgeist of the 1920s; she rein-vented her boyish styles in the 1950s to see them becoming defining silhouettes of the 1960s. The collarless cardigan-style suit is one of the great success stories of the modern age and has been much copied, especially in the 1980s, and will remain a perennial classic for ladies of all ages. Under the stewardship of Karl Lagerfeld, the House of Chanel goes from strength to strength.

GLAMOUR

Glamour is always a good look too, but it can intimidate people sometimes. Not necessarily a bad thing, but something to keep in mind—perhaps that's why pulling out the stops is generally reserved for the evening, rather than a trip to the supermarket.

Glamour is most appropriate at the cocktail party, the theatre, ballet or opera: it appreciates a sense of occasion, of drama. Dress like a Hollywood movie star or famous model in floor- or tea-length gown and sparkly accessories. To ramp it up even more—add gloves. Nothing says glamour better than gloves—and you can enjoy taking them off at suitable opportunities.

Grooming is key for glamour—as it is for elegance—so ensure your hair is looking fabulous and indulge in some strong make up too.

Ignore the killjoys who haven't made an effort—you're brightening up the world and setting the standard.

Glamour is a magic spell you cast about you to entice and enthral—glamour takes your look into another bold and beautiful world where you stand out and make the most of what you have.

Glamour helps you feel strong and confident. It's a weapon against the world, to protect you while inviting in those you choose. It can be bold, sexy and sometimes brash, but should never be crass.

Glamour is a simple and effective style—perhaps a red lipstick is all that it takes, or an impractically high heel. The swish of a full skirt. It's an awareness of the artificiality of life, how nature is fine but can benefit from a little improvement, and there's no harm in revealing your efforts to enhance your looks.

It can entail embracing lingerie: not just for its practical and sensual characteristics, but also for its structural potential to cinch the waist, propel the bust, curve the hips or smooth your figure with a petticoat, girdle or even corset.

The queens of glamour are the Golden Era of Hollywood movie stars—life was never dull for these ladies, in their ballgowns and expertly coiffured hair. They never left the house without a full face of make up and the prettiest of shoes, always ready for their close up, but the look is an easily emulated one, without being so high maintenance.

Good examples of the style are early screen siren Jean Harlow with her platinum-blonde curls (the most glamorous of hair colours) and satin bias-cut gowns. Her hair was expertly coloured and then worn in a soft and short Marcel wave style that framed her face. Cupid bow red lips and arched brows— make up should never be forgotten in your search for style.

Hollywood provides many examples of glamour—Marilyn Monroe epitomised the 1950s adoration of the feminine figure, with dresses that exaggerated her copious curves, more platinum hair and red lips. Her eyes were highlighted with winged eyeliner—Marilyn was an expert make up artist, mixing three shades of lipstick to produce her own special blend.

In the eighteenth-century tradition, Marilyn applied eyebrow pencil to a facial mole as a slight imperfection highlights the perfection of the rest of her face. Just one mole: she had two but the other was concealed with foundation. Her mole, which also bestowed vulnerability, has become the identifying feature of her iconic face, reoccurring in the sea of imitators.

In the 1960s Brigitte Bardot displayed a more girlish, relaxed kind of glamour with ballet flats—and ballet grace and posture too—with gingham Capri pants, worn with simple tops and a sultry disdainful pout. Attitude can be an important part of your look (but only if authentic).

Dusty Springfield brought glamour to the microphone with her thick, blonde bouffant and pale pink lipstick, as did Ronnie Spector and the 1960s girl groups—a look reinvented in modern times by Amy Winehouse.

Amy's look combined elements of 1950s pulp fiction style (tight pencil skirts, cleavage baring tops) with a dash of 1960s–80s Mod style with Fred Perry polo tops. Trashier than most glamour looks, it maintained the artificiality and hyper femininity and yet was accessible. Sailor-style tattoos, a Marilyn mole and an overblown Ronettes bouffant updated the look.

In the 1970s Jerry Hall and Bianca Jagger provided disco-style glamour with slinky, polyester-knit, Grecian-style goddess dresses with plunging necklines and thigh-high splits revealing tanned legs and stiletto heels.

Gwen Stefani borrows liberally from her platinum blonde, bombshell predecessors—her tall, lithe frame perfectly suited to 1930s styles, but she is also a true fashion originator, borrowing from Japanese Harajuku Lolita styles and elements from many eras including current trends. She is bold and courageous, knowing well what works for her figure—which is almost everything (lucky lady). No doubt the many women in her family who are seamstresses helped give her confidence with clothes and experimental fashion from a young age.

Gwen always wears a flawless vintage-inspired make up look—clean, porcelain complexion, strong lips and long black eyelashes. She favours the striking hair of Harlow, and was even cast as her role model in Martin Scorsese's film *The Aviator* (2004).

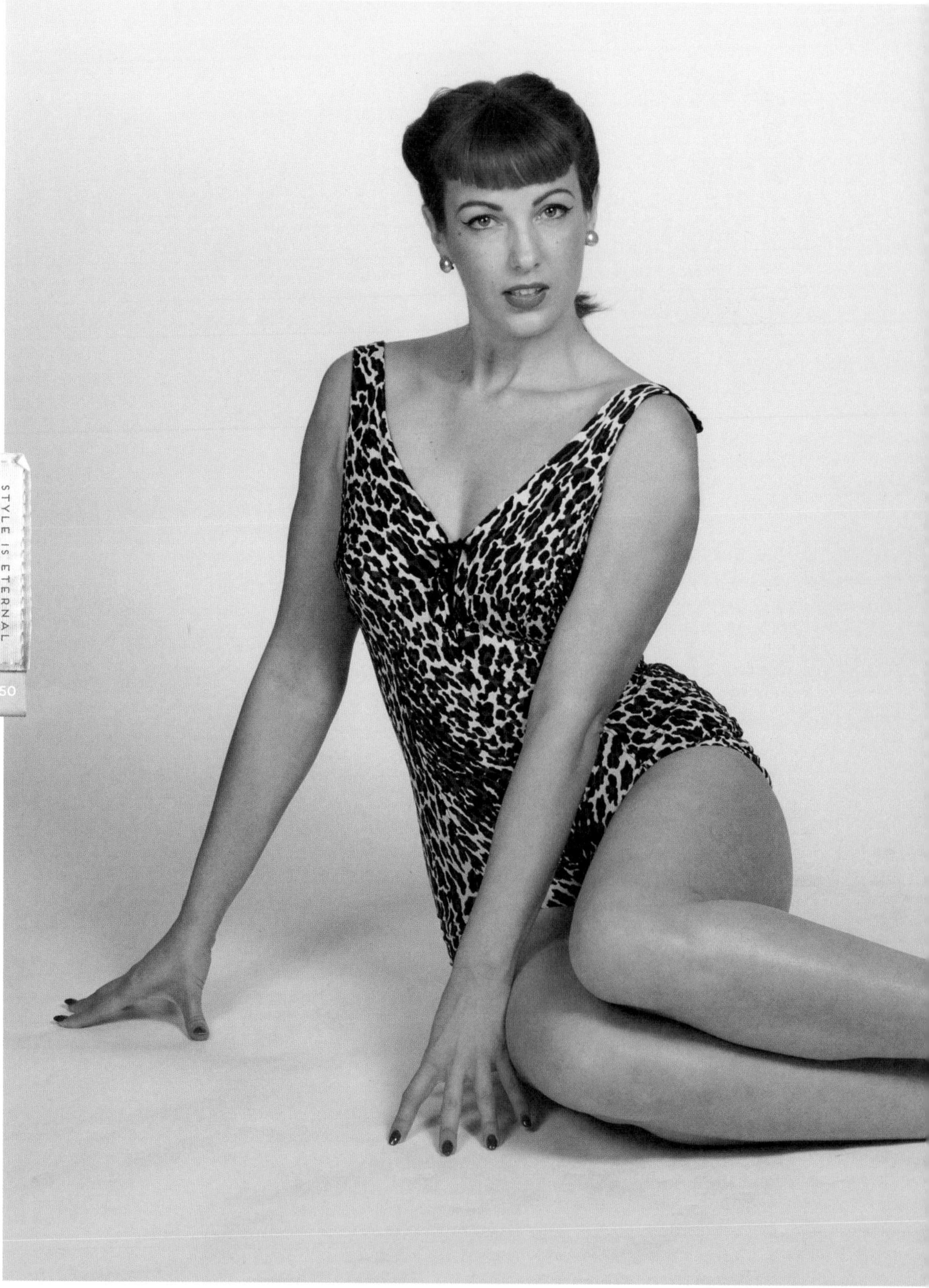

FUN

Dressing up isn't just about being a fabulous grown up—you can also indulge a sense of playfulness and wit. It's nice to be beautiful but how much better is it to be interesting?

Think Elsa Schiaparelli with her surrealist fashions of the late 1930s, like her hat shaped like a shoe, or silk dress printed with *trompe l'oeil* fabric rips, or quilted skeleton bones. I'm sure those items fuelled conversation at the time, and we're still talking about them more than seventy years later.

Carmen Miranda in the 1940s was one who embraced colour and vibrancy with oversized hats piled high with tropical fruits, her full, ruffled skirts parting to reveal enormous platform shoes as she swayed and sang salsas.

Lucille Ball was our greatest TV comedienne in the 1950s with polka dot dresses with full skirts, petticoats and cute aprons in her show *I Love Lucy*. One of the great slapstick artists, she always managed to look good while entertaining us.

Fun is a great way to enjoy more casual events like pool parties or picnics—big, floppy hats with vintage-style sunglasses, childlike accessories and bright colours. Wicker picnic baskets with polka dot linings and full skirts with petticoats for sprawling on the grass.

ROMANCE

Don't you need more romance in your life? Romance can happen anywhere—it's the way you feel when you're doing something that appeals to your senses.

It's in a beautiful floral fabric that makes you feel like spring is just around the corner and in impractical but irresistible shoes that you can barely walk in, but which look awfully nice as you perch on a stool in a French patisserie sipping *chocolat chaud*.

Romance is there at the High Tea party when you're wearing your favourite lace frock, with your mint-green handbag and that adorable little cocktail hat you picked up at the vintage fair.

Romance is there as you reach for the macaron that matches the colour of your antique tea cup so perfectly—you gaze contentedly at your well-dressed friends and all is well in the world.

Part of the great joy of being a woman is the ability to indulge in femininity: be romantic and play up your charms with full skirts, floral prints, soft and sensual fabrics like velvets and lace that invite cuddles and compliments.

Reveal the shape of your body in styles that emphasise your bust, waist, hips, legs or bum—or if you prefer, your well toned arms and lovely hands—this can be done through your choice of sleeve and jewellery, to bring attention to the areas you are most confident with.

This look is most successful when only one part of your body is highlighted: perhaps a tiny waist, but please resist the urge to show off your spectacular bosom at the same time, as it dilutes the lady-like effect.

Doris Day in the 1950s provided a demure counterpoint to the glamorous stars of the day with her neat and pretty looks, with flowing skirts, chiffons and a sunny smile.

WARDROBE ANALYSIS

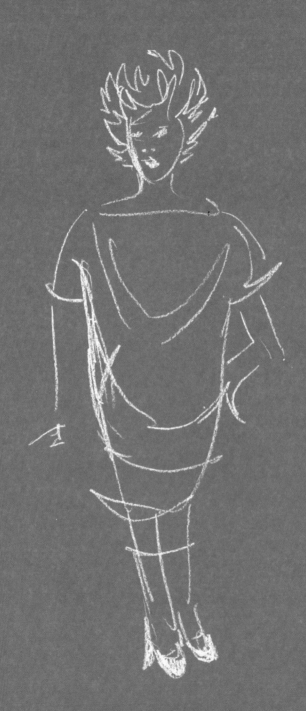

What you want from your wardrobe changes as your life does. To optimise wardrobe space, regular analysis of your wardrobe will help you see where additions and changes are needed. Every piece in your wardrobe needs to earn its keep.

You should have a roughly equal number of items for spring/summer and autumn/winter. Evidently, there should be an adequate supply of everything you need day-to-day: clothes for work, clothes for relaxing, going out, sport and events.

Now, go through your wardrobe and pull out anything that you haven't worn in over a year and ask yourself, how come? Be honest: unless it's a special occasion piece, it's probably something you don't need. Do you want it in your wardrobe? Create a pile for clothes that are past their usefulness.

Also pull out anything that you did wear, but that has had its moment in the sun and is no longer appealing; time to pass it on to someone else—it, too, can go onto the 'unwanted' pile.

Then sort out the rest into types—dresses all together here; tops there; jackets and coats in another spot; and skirts and pants also together. This will make the next step easier: try everything on. If it doesn't fit or flatter you or needs repairs, ask yourself if improving it would make a difference? If not, onto the 'unwanted' pile. Don't keep anything that doesn't fit and can't be altered to fit; but if it can be improved, put it into a second pile. Be ruthless, there's no room in your life for clothes you don't wear or want to wear.

The rest can go back into your wardrobe for the moment.

Have a whip through the 'improve' pile to evaluate pieces for repairs and potential alterations: is it up to a second life? It's not always worthwhile to fix a garment—the cost may be higher than simply buying a replacement, or it may be beyond saving if the fabric has deteriorated or sustained significant damage. If it looks like a no, send it into the 'unwanted' pile.

If it's a yes, organise for you or someone else to do the work. Be a woman of action: the longer you leave it, the more likely it is that these items will end up as unwanteds too.

It's so easy to be sentimental about our clothes—they carry our precious memories, but if they've outlived their usefulness in your wardrobe, send them back out into the world where someone else can enjoy them; they're made to be worn, not languish in a wardrobe.

Op shops are pleased to receive donations in good condition—so make sure they're clean and have no major issues, or they'll end up in the rag bin.

If you are getting rid of clothing of good quality, you may also be able to recover some of your investment. Some options for selling your unwanted fashions include holding a garage sale, renting a stall at a second-hand fashion market or flea market; selling or consigning to second-hand shops; selling via online marketplaces; or offering them to your friends and network through social media.

Keep in mind that the more effort you put in, the better the price you're likely to get. You'll also get the best price selling directly to the new wearer rather than to someone who takes a cut to on-sell for you, like a retailer.

MAINTENANCE

Perhaps you have a mending pile and the skill to maintain it, but find that time always gets away from you? Schedule a little time to set up your equipment, have a drink ready and some nice music—you'll find it can be a pleasure—or perhaps organise a sewing bee with your friends?

While everyone should have a basic sewing kit and be able to maintain their wardrobe with simple repairs like sewing on buttons and fixing hems, if you lack the skills, time or inclination, find a professional you can rely on. Always ask for a quote and timeframe before agreeing to any work.

Now that you have a—probably smaller—wardrobe of pieces that work for you, find out if they work for each other! The next step is to see if they all coordinate.

Dresses can go to one side: they're instant outfits that need nothing more than accessories as extras.

Jackets can be worn over dresses and tops—make sure they all improve what they are worn over. Mix them along seasonal lines: linen jackets over summer dresses, not woollen knits. Clashing can work, but neutral colours are reliable combiners and make great basics. Try mixing patterns, especially if they share a colour scheme. See what works and build your confidence.

Every top needs to go with at least one of your bottoms, but preferably two or three. Likewise, every bottom should suit an array of tops. When you identify those loved pieces that lack playmates, it should be fairly obvious what you need to acquire to complete an outfit—start a list.

Depending on your climate, you're likely to need at a minimum one good coat of a suitable weight. Are you holding on to that lovely, full-length, mohair coat that looks great on, but that you never wear because you live in the tropics? Perhaps a shawl or wrap will be better for those rare cool nights.

If you find that you have wonderful dressy clothes that you're not getting any use out of, perhaps you need to go out more? All you need is a well-dressed companion, and you can go almost anywhere. Cocktail bars, afternoon tea and picnics are good opportunities to frock up.

At the end of this process you should have a list of what you need to fill the gaps. When adding to your wardrobe, look for quality, and remember that when buying new, you get what you pay for. If you can't afford something, consider whether you will be able to pick it up in the sales (keeping in mind that it may not be available in your size or colour any more), or perhaps find a second-hand version that is likely to be much cheaper. Popular designer items sell for much less second-hand.

I believe in buying the right piece when you find it, even if you have to stretch the budget. While you were waiting for the sale you could have been wearing it, and when the time comes you may be looking for the next season's fashions anyway. Sales tend to take the gloss off an item, and a retail experience too.

GOOD BUYS

Shopping locally is just one of many ways to add to your wardrobe—here are some more options for finding what you're looking for.

SHOPPING ONLINE

The wonderful world of the internet offers the shopper more options than ever before: you can analyse your favourite shop's new range without leaving home, or see what they have on sale. If you already know something works for you, it's an easy way to check out what other colours it comes in or which styles from the range might coordinate well.

Don't limit yourself to national retailers: have a look at what is available overseas, as many items are not stocked locally and the changes in season mean that you can often buy out-of-season for cost savings.

GUIDE TO MEASUREMENTS AND SIZES

BUST Measure round fullest part of bust.

WAIST Measure round natural waistline.

HIPS Measure round widest part of hips.

LENGTH Measure from neck to hemline.

NECK Measure neck where collar normally fits.

TROUSERS Down inside seam from crutch to cuff bottom.

WAIST Over trouser waistband without belt.

CHEST high under arms and over shoulder blades.

ONLINE SHOPPING TIPS

⬚ Ensure that you're ordering the right size to avoid returns. Look for a sizing chart or measurements and allow extra space to fit: for example, if your bust measures 90 cm, look for a size that is at least 2–3 cm larger. It helps to measure something similar from your wardrobe that fits you well. Choose the size that fits the largest part of your body as the item can be taken in or cinched with a belt if needed. For example, I have large biceps after years of driving big vintage cars without power steering, so I often have to go up a size or two to accommodate them if the sleeves are fitted.

⬚ Read the shipping charges. Some online sellers include free shipping, but most will charge you postage and maybe a handling fee, and some will inflate these charges to make up for an item sold below cost. Make sure that you know what you're up for before hitting the checkout. Consider insurance, registered post and tracking to avoid your purchase getting lost in the mail.

⬚ Choose a delivery address that is manned during the day—this could be your work or a friend's place if you won't be home, or ask them to leave it on the doorstep if you're happy to take the risk. Another option is a post-office box, which has the added bonus of protecting your privacy.

⬚ If the colour is important, look for a written description as well as photos—monitors can change the way an image appears and it can be disappointing to receive orange when you expected red. Contact the seller if no information is provided.

⬚ Look for care instructions—you might prefer an item that's machine washable rather than dry clean only; this information should be available on the product page.

⬚ Check their refund policy—just like regular shops, webstores have an obligation to offer refunds according to the legislation in their location. Your state's Consumer Affairs web-site will provide more information. Different laws apply in other countries, and you will probably have to pay return shipping unless the fault is with them. Some online sellers make up their own rules—check before you buy to avoid disappointment.

▨ If you're purchasing vintage fashion, carefully read all details pertaining to condition. 'Item not as described' is the biggest reason for returns with second-hand goods. Even vintage clothing that is 'new old stock' or 'deadstock', while unworn, may have sustained damage through poor storage. Assume nothing.

▨ Buy from professional sellers—the likelihood of your having a positive experience is greatly increased by dealing with someone who knows what they're doing and can be trusted. Sadly, there are shysters and amateurs online who will happily take your money and run.

▨ Look for 'https' in the URL of webpages that process payments. This represents a secure certificate, which is your guarantee that your financial details are safe. If you don't see this, find another way to purchase their products. PayPal is one such method and most sellers will accept if asked. Other options include over the phone, in person or by email (note that this is not very secure, so use caution with credit card details).

▨ When you click 'buy' to finalise payment, only click on it once, even if it's taking a while to process—clicking twice could process multiple payments, which can take several days to be refunded.

▨ Ask any questions you have, no matter how trivial—some sites offer live customer service for immediate responses, but even small artisanal shops are happy to answer questions and normally respond quickly.

Buying online is no substitute for the experience of going into a shop, seeing and touching the whole range, or trying on different sizes while being served by a capable assistant. Plus you can take your purchases home right away, no waiting for the postman. Even better, put them on and walk out in your new fashions!

LET'S GO SHOPPING

We're all familiar with buying clothes in retail environments, but are you getting the most out of your experience? Here are some ways to increase the likelihood of bagging something good.

⊠ Dress for the day. Wear comfortable and crease-resistant clothes that can be easily taken off. Separates are ideal, as you only need to partially undress, depending on what you're trying on. Wear easy-to-remove shoes rather than boots for the same reason.

⊠ Wear nice underwear. You're probably going to be looking at yourself in harsh lighting, so wear underwear that won't compel you to add it to your shopping list and will sit flatly under the clothes you're trying on. Lighter and skin-tone undergarments are best, as they don't show through sheerer fabrics.

⊠ When selecting a size to try on, take the two either side of yours so you don't need to make two trips. Sizes vary a great deal between brands and styles, so there's no need to stress if your regular size doesn't fit. If a size tag really bothers you, you can always remove it at home.

⊠ Try on the largest size first. It's much quicker to try on something that may be too big rather than something that could be too small, and it's a more pleasant surprise to find you need something smaller.

⊠ Try something different. Don't just stick to the usual colours and styles. There's nothing lost, and you might find you like it.

⊠ Be nice to the sales staff. Retail can be a challenging and physically demanding occupation, and even the best people have bad moments, so please don't judge them too harshly. If you have an issue with the service you receive, ask to speak to their manager or submit a complaint through the website.

BUYING VINTAGE

'Vintage fashion' is a term that describes fashion of a previous era (generally pre-1965 or 1990 depending on who you ask). It's a term that has caché, particularly in the category of evening wear, where it offers high-class glamour at a cut-price rate.

Note that the term is also confusingly used to describe brand new, modern fashion that is reminiscent of an earlier era, but to differentiate I call these styles 'vintage reproduction' or 'vintage style'.

Authentic vintage fashion is usually (but not always) second-hand and is one of the world's oldest trades, flourishing today more than ever. It offers the discerning fashion lover an unlimited range of styles, regardless of current trends. In general, the rarer an item is, the more sought after it is: good condition is also important.

In contrast to vintage fashion where age increases the value, second-hand designer fashion is most valued when it is less than two years old. These pieces originally came with high price tags, but with a little searching, you can pick them up at a fraction of the price. You also get the benefit of styles that may be sold out or are rare. Second-hand designer wear makes a much better investment than the new product too, which loses value as soon it is popped into that lovely carry bag and walked out the door.

The third type of second-hand clothing is the largest category—items that are not particularly old or interesting but still have plenty of life in them, discarded by the owner because of some small issue or no longer fitting. These are the fashions you'll find at op shops, and they can offer a very cost effective solution while also being good for the environment.

WHERE TO BUY VINTAGE

☒ second-hand shops

☒ markets and vintage fairs

☒ garage sales

☒ webstores and online marketplaces

☒ from friends and family—the very traditional 'hand me downs'

Always inspect second-hand clothing for moth and insect damage and try to avoid damaged pieces unless you really love them and they can be repaired. Make sure you wash or dry clean any potentially affected item before introducing it to your wardrobe, as eggs or larvae may be hidden in the fibres.

When buying vintage, designer and second-hand fashion, keep in mind that rarity is an important part of the appeal— so hesitating to purchase may mean losing out.

Second-hand fashion of all types is innately environmentally friendly, as you're not contributing to any of the negative issues associated with fashion production while saving an item from possible ragging or landfill. It's the greenest fashion of all.

GOOD BUYS

QUALITY NOT QUANTITY

I t's so tempting to fill our wardrobes with bright, shiny new things to play with. But no matter how many clothes you have, you are likely to wear the same small selection of pieces over and over again—the rest becomes 'stuff' that clogs up your storage and saps your energy.

Choose your pieces carefully and maintain them in good condition, and they will reward you with many years of use.

Caring for your wardrobe is of the utmost importance. Even the best and most expensive items will let you down—and look shabby to others—if they're not clean and in good condition. Conversely, your clothes may be old or cheap but can look good as long as they're clean and well kept.

It is a legal requirement that new garments come with care instructions and these should be adhered to as much as possible, although some smaller companies and dressmaker items still do not include them. Second-hand clothes may have had the labels removed, so, in case you find yourself with something that you're not sure how to treat, it can be helpful to have a rudimentary knowledge of how to clean all types of clothes.

Most fabrics can be washed—the gentle cycle on your machine is best, as it isn't as rough on the textiles. The cleaning process is what causes the most deterioration to clothes, so it's best to treat them gently.

Hand washing or dry cleaning is recommended for anything with delicate detailing—including lace, beading, embroidery and sequins. Anything you hand wash should be dried on a line or, if the item is heavily embellished, gently squeeze out excess water and dry flat on a towel. These items will be pulled out of shape in a dryer or hanging on a line, although when almost dry, you can place them over the line for a good airing.

If hand washing wool (for example, knitwear or an un-lined jacket, trousers or skirt) keep the water temperature warm, as water that's too hot can permanently felt the wool and shrink it. Tailored wool garments should be drycleaned.

DRY CLEAN ONLY

⊠ Satins, taffetas and acetate linings lose their crispness when washed.

⊠ Delicate materials and those that are heavily embellished with beads or sequins are likely to be damaged when washed.

⊠ Printed silks—the print may not be colourfast and could run.

⊠ Silk chiffons and georgettes are delicate materials and easy to damage during laundering.

⊠ Velvets become crushed if washed.

⊠ Crepes (rayon, silk or polyester) can shrink when washed. Silk crepe is a strong material and can sometimes be steamed back into shape, but rayon will likely rip.

⊠ Tailored and lined garments contain more than one fabric type and one may shrink slightly during laundering, pulling the delicate balance of the style out of whack.

STAIN REMOVAL

If stains on your garment don't come out with your usual laundry routine, they'll need special attention. If you can identify the cause of the mark (pen, or red wine, for example), apply a specialist product from your supermarket. Take care, as spot removal can remove dye from surrounding areas, leaving you with a larger problem. If in doubt, seek advice, as it is easy to ruin something by applying the wrong treatment.

Cottons, rayons, viscoses, linens and polyesters can be soaked in oxygen bleach and the hottest water they can take. Cottons and linens can take very hot water (less for colours). Rayons and viscoses require cooler temperatures—see the care label for recommendations. Those that shouldn't be soaked are silks, wools, tailored items or items containing more than one fabric type, such as a lined skirt.

For stained dry clean only items, consider whether they can indeed be washed—washing and soaking is much more effective in removing marks than dry cleaning. If it must be dry cleaned, see your specialist for stain removal.

Always try to follow the care label, although with experience you can learn how to handle certain fabrics effectively with a wider range of treatments. Care labels tend to err on the side of caution.

If a spot won't come out there are ways you can hide it. Consider disguising the mark by covering it with detailing—beadwork, embroidery, appliqués, ribbons, lace or other trims. You could cover it with patchwork or a panel of lace, chiffon or other fabric. You might be able to patch it using surplus fabric from facings or pockets. You can also cut out damage and make it a feature like a keyhole opening. Basically, as long as the fabric is strong, you can always work around it. Note that any opening cut into the fabric should be finished off properly with a facing or binding or it will fray after being washed.

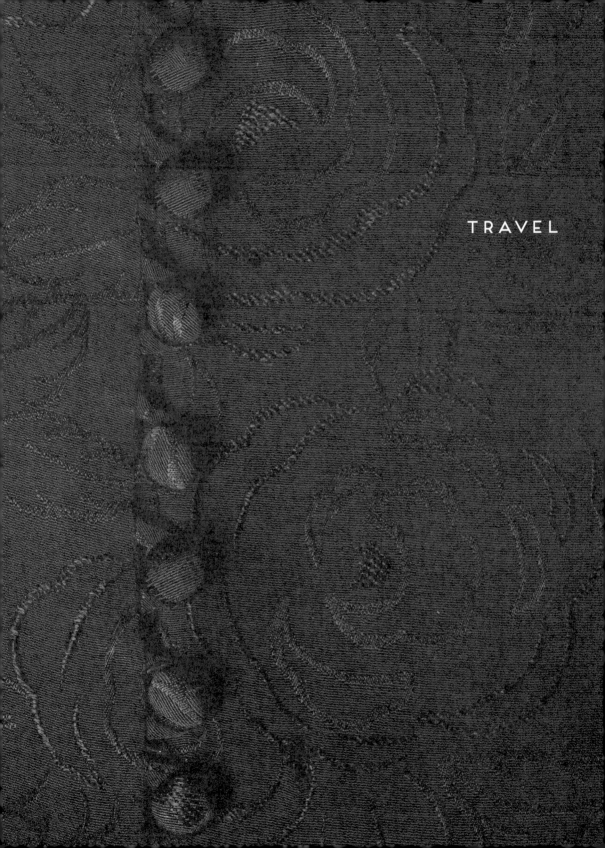

TRAVEL

Travel is a great opportunity to concentrate your style into a small and serviceable mini-wardrobe.

The best travel advice I ever heard was to 'halve your clothes and double your money'. The more I travel, the more I appreciate travelling light—and buying anything I need while away. Fashion makes wonderful souvenirs too.

Everything you take you will have to carry, sometimes a longer way than you expect—I once packed up a small vintage hat-box for a trip across the country for a family funeral. It was a pretty little thing, lined in tartan and trimmed in ribbons and I easily filled it with all that I needed for a week away. Unfortunately, when arriving late at night at the country train station I found taxis in short supply and had to walk the several miles to my hotel. By the time I got there, I had decided that never again would I prioritise style over practicality when travelling.

There's no reason you can't have both though, with a little thought—start with the case, and choose the smallest and lightest you can fit everything into. A good guide is the carry-on limit for aircraft—it's such an advantage to avoid checking in luggage, leaving the airport as soon as you've arrived at the other end. There are many nice options available in this size, and a solid form (rather than a soft backpack) enables firm packing and protection of interior items. Make sure it's not too heavy for the cabin limit.

Look for a bag that is unusual enough to easily identify on the baggage carousel if you check it in, or, if it's plain, add a ribbon or decal or some feature to make it stand out—you don't want to waste time when you're exhausted after a long flight.

The great advantage of your travel wardrobe is that the people you're seeing are unlikely to be with you every day, so there's no harm in wearing a small number of items multiple times as long as they're clean—you should be able to wash as you go along. Only take items that coordinate well together so you can get maximum use out of them—accessories can help basics go a lot further.

Regardless of where you travel, you will always need at least two pairs of shoes—so that you can allow them to dry out between wears, and also so you won't find yourself in a pickle if your one pair lets you down. I once found myself in a small town on a public holiday needing a new pair of shoes as the heel came off the ones I wore. Not ideal.

Many people dress down on holiday, which is a great pity—I always dress up, wearing heels and lipstick even if I'm only spending the day in the hotel lounge. You choose to stay in nice surroundings, so shouldn't you dress to suit them? I always think dressing up ensures better service from staff and other guests smile upon you too. A nice bonus is that your holiday snaps are more likely to be flattering if you're looking and feeling your best.

MY THREE-WEEKS-IN-PARIS WINTER WARDROBE

- ☒ black jersey dress
- ☒ black-and-white polka-dot dress
- ☒ black, high-waisted, box-pleat skirt
- ☒ olive-green, cotton men's shirt (can be worn open as a light jacket over a dress)
- ☒ burgundy, fine-knit wool, V neck jumper (wear over dresses, shirt or by itself as a top)
- ☒ black stretch jeans
- ☒ black high heels
- ☒ black boots for walking
- ☒ black, wool, 1960s pea coat
- ☒ underwear, hosiery, beret, gloves and scarves

I wore the bulkiest items on the flight and packed the rest into a small vanity case, including a fold-out fabric bag for shopping, a portable hairdryer and mini sizes of toiletries. Every night I washed out the lingerie, hosiery and items of clothing that needed washing—shampoo can double as detergent when space is at a premium.

Black makes an excellent base, as do neutrals. The last time I travelled to Paris I packed camel as the base colour, which also worked well.

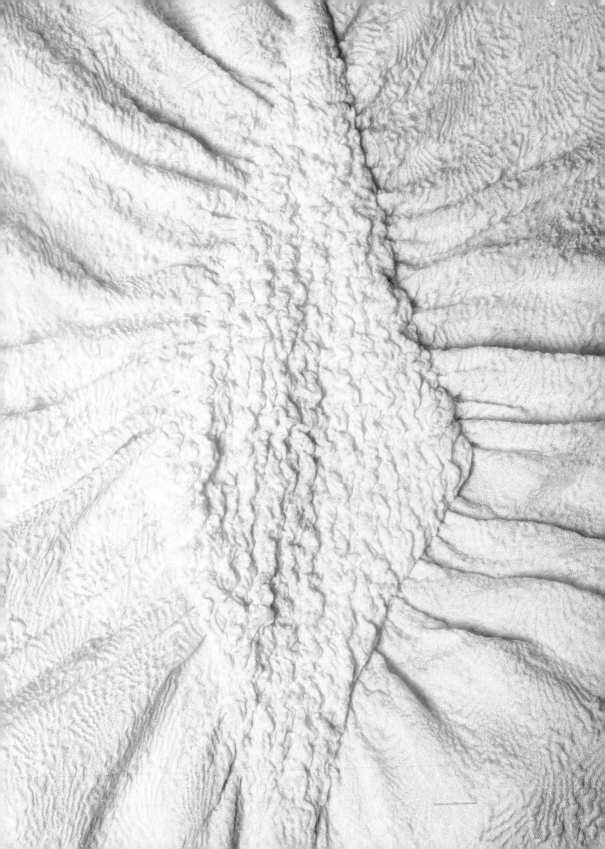

MIXING NEW AND VINTAGE

Y ou've now got a good idea of some of the options available with fashion and how particular styles will work to your advantage—now is the time to put them together with some twists and see how well they work for you.

Remember that current fashion always leans heavily on the back catalogue of previous styles for inspiration. Be ahead of the pack by reading trends and seeking quality originals to create a unique look.

For example, floral 1930s and 1940s style frocks are coming back into fashion—the last time they were popular was in the 1990s, and they can be picked up easily and economically from vintage and op shops. Bonus points for rayon and cotton versions that wear better than polyester and look nicer too. They can be matched with a 1950s-style cardigan, now a mass-produced fashion staple, in any colour.

The late 1970s is also a major trend, with hand-tooled leather handbags—originals are available from flea markets—and boho jackets and jeans. 1960s styles are perennial favourites with so many different trends to choose from—feminine *Mad Men* floral frocks to sleek *2001: A Space Odyssey*-style Mod, to richly textured ethnic looks—current fashion is always dipping into this decade. The more simple and elegant Audrey Hepburn-influenced styles were favourites for office workers in the 1990s and are easily picked up around the traps too.

Cyndi Lauper and Madonna indulged in the vintage dress up box for their fun and sexy early 1980s looks that mixed 1950s with contemporary fashion, and underwear as outerwear, a look that inspired Jean Paul Gaultier to create his iconic conical bras and corsetry in the 1990s.

Courtney Love and Kate Moss look to 1930s femininity for evening wear looks and every day glamour, while stars like Julia Roberts made headlines in vintage Valentino couture.

ACKNOWLEDGEMENTS

Thank you to Melbourne University Publishing and the wonderful and talented people who helped me bring this book to life: Sally Heath, Cathy Smith, Penelope White, Lily Keil, Louise Stirling, Terri King and Monica Svarc.

Thank you to designer Trisha Garner for taking those words and turning them into an elegant book filled with colour, texture, beautiful fashion and interesting people.

Thank you to Frankie Valentine for letting me dress you in fashion from 1920s to the current day, and to Dominic Deacon for photography and editing. Thank you to Anna Young for help on the shoot.

The demands of this book have been fitted around the busy schedule of my shop, Circa Vintage Clothing, and wouldn't have been possible without the assistance of my colleagues Esther Hayes, Clare St Clare and Becky Lou. Thank you.

Fashions from my personal collection and Circa feature in this book, and for that I thank the many people who have entrusted their treasures to me over the last thirty years.

I'd also like to thank the late Geoff Walker, who provided the archival images from his collection of vintage mail order catalogues.

Thank you to my literary agent Clare Forster at Curtis Brown, and to Tanya Ha for the introduction.

Most of all, thank you to my husband Tim Hamilton for his love and support, my late mother Denny, who instilled in me a love of fashion from a young age and my father Brian for permission to reproduce a family photograph.

CAPTIONS

p. iv silk shantung dress with guipure lace (detail), circa early 1960s; **p. ix** cotton floral print dress with broderie anglaise trim, circa late 1930s as worn by the author in 1969; **p. x** silk and metallic lamé bias cut wedding gown (detail), circa late 1930s; **p. 1** cotton petticoat with ruffle and rope hem (detail), circa late 1950s; **p. 3** silk satin and lace petticoat (detail), circa late 1940s; **p. 4** silk crepe floral bias cut tea gown with draped and open shoulders, circa early 1930s; **p. 5** satchel style floral handbag, circa 2010s; **p. 6** silver beaded silk evening top (detail), circa early 1990s; **p. 7** accordion pleated 'goddess' evening gown (detail), circa early 1970s; **p. 9** bias cut dress with clutch handbag, circa 1930s; **p. 11** striped blouse with full sleeves, circa 1940s; **p. 12** cotton shift dress with contrast top-stitching (detail), circa late 1960s; **p. 13** chiffon evening gown with beaded ruched waistband (detail), circa mid 1960s; **p. 15** silk shantung dress with guipure lace (detail), circa early 1960s; **p. 17** cotton lace fitted shift dress with empire line bust and notched neckline, circa early 1960s; **pp. 18–19** fitted evening gown with diamante ring and starburst diamante detailing, circa late 1960s; **p. 29** cotton print playsuit with elastic shirring and built-in bra, circa late 1950s; **p. 30** silk shantung fitted shell top circa early 1960s with high-waisted pencil skirt circa late 1970s; **p. 32** polka dot top with shoulder pads, circa 1980s; **p. 33** silver beaded silk top, circa early 1990s; **p. 34** beaded lambswool cardigan, circa late 1950s with wool pencil skirt, circa late 1970s; **p. 39** cotton shift dress with inverted box pleats and contrast top-stitching (detail), circa late 1960s; **p. 40** printed chiffon palazzo pants with knife pleats, circa late 1980s; **p. 45** cotton overalls with sailor style blouse, circa 1930s; **p. 47** blouses with fitted short shorts, circa 1930s; **p. 49** acrylic faux fur gilet, circa 2010s; **p. 51** blazer with notched collar and striped scarf, circa 2010s; **p. 53** fitted linen dress with tucked bodice and matching bolero jacket, circa 1980s; **p. 54** silk chinoise hand-embroidered coat, circa 1920s; **p. 59** cape with collar and shoulder pads, circa early 1940s; **p. 62** rhinestone neckline, circa 1940s; **p. 63** crownless hat with upturned brim, circa early 1940s; **p. 69** silk and metallic lamé skirt with mink collar and lizardskin handbag, circa early 1960s; **pp. 70–1** lace 1950s style dress with clutch bag, circa 2010s; **p. 73** fitted jacket with scarf, circa

2000s; **p. 74** pillbox hat and Peter Pan collar, circa mid 1960s; **p. 75** bathing beauties wearing swimwear and accessories, circa 1930s; **p. 77** ostrich feather capelet, gloves and cocktail hat, circa 1930s; **p.78** (top) calfskin gauntlet style gloves, circa early 1960s, (bottom) jacket, floral blouse, sunglasses and leather gloves with pearl necklace worn as bracelet, circa 2010s; **p.79** matching fine wool coat, silk head scarf and gauntlet style gloves with mother of pearl buttons, circa 1930s; **p. 82** seamed fishnet 1940s style stockings, circa 2010s; **p. 87** court shoes and stockings, circa 1930s; **p. 88** velvet vest with buttoned half-belt (detail), circa late 1960s; **p. 89** rayon jacquard and lace bedjacket (detail), circa 1940s; **p. 91** printed cotton dress (detail), circa early 1970s; **p. 93** cotton print 'Victorian revival' tiered maxi dress, circa early 1970s; **pp. 94–5** chiffon evening gown, circa mid 1960s; **p. 97** cotton abstract floral print A-line sundress with centre front zipper, circa late 1960s; **p. 98** cotton and lace 1950s style dress with full skirt and collar, circa 1990s; **p. 100** plain dinner dress, circa 1930s; **p. 101** cotton print playsuit with elastic shirring and built-in bra, circa late 1950s; **p. 102** printed 1940s style cotton dress with sash, circa early 1970s; **pp. 104–5** printed nylon dress with rhinestone buckle and cotton, tulle and lace crinoline petticoats, circa 1950s; **pp. 108–9** Iris Apfel wearing structured dress with necklaces and bracelets and her signature oversized glasses, circa 2010s; **p. 110** 1950s style spectacle frames, circa 2010s; **p. 111** silk wedding gown, circa 1930s; **p. 112** silk satin and lace nightgown (detail), circa late 1930s; **p. 113** printed cotton voile and crepe maxi dress (detail), circa early 1970s; **p. 116** crepe dinner dress with ribbon and bead trim to the bodice and knife pleated skirt, circa late 1930s; **p. 117** strapless rose printed silk party dress, circa early 1950s; **p. 118** silk and wool alaskine evening dress with metallic threads, circa late 1960s; **pp. 120–1** Henry VIII, circa 1490s; **p. 121** Elizabeth I, circa 1500s; **p. 122** bias cut maxi dress with lace up back, circa mid 1970s; **p. 124** accordion pleated 'goddess' evening gown with lettuce leaf hem, circa early 1970s; **p. 127** man-style tailcoat with formal vest and top hat, circa 1930s; **p. 132** leisure wear with knitted vests, skirt and lace up Oxford style shoes, circa 1940s; **p. 136** silk and wool alaskine evening dress with metallic (detail), circa late 1960s; **p. 137** silk jacquard cheong sam dress (detail), circa 1960s; **p. 139** evening set with midriff top, high collar and long train trimmed in marabou feathers, circa 1930s; **p. 140** silk georgette dress with cut steel beadwork, circa early 1940s; **p. 141** crepe evening dress with silver beads, circa early 1960s; **pp. 142–3** Karl Lagerfeld and models at a Chanel fashion parade, 2011; **p. 144** Marilyn Monroe wearing metallic evening gown, 1953; **p. 145** Louise Brooks wearing silk and metallic evening gown, circa 1920s; **p. 146** Joan Crawford wearing silk two-tone evening gown in the film *Letty Lynton*, 1932; **p. 147** wrap style boudoir gown with oversized tassels, circa late 1930s; **p. 148** (top) Amy Winehouse wearing ruched top and hair rose, 2007, (bottom) Gwen Stefani wearing sequinned evening gown with plunging neckline, 2011; **p. 149** silk metallic sarong dress with matching stole, circa 1960s; **p. 150** leopard print swimsuit with lace up bodice, circa early 1970s; **p. 152** printed rayon and rubber swimsuit with high heel shoes, circa late 1930s; **p. 153** silk taffeta, lace and tulle ballgown, circa early 1950s; **p. 154** tulle party dress with guipure lace and diamantes (detail), circa 1950s; **p. 155** velvet evening gown with rosette (detail), circa 1980s; **p. 159** silk crepe evening gown with shoulder pads and keyhole neckline, circa 1940s; **p. 162** embroidered silk blouse (detail) circa mid 1960s; **p. 163** silk satin evening dress with shirred bodice (detail), circa mid 1930s; **p. 169** printed cotton voile tea gown with sweetheart neckline and circle skirt, circa late 1930s; **p. 171** silk satin evening dress with shirred bodice, circa late 1930s; **p. 172** silk chiffon and devoré velvet drop waisted tea gown, circa late 1920s; **p. 174** printed cotton voile tea gown (detail), circa late 1930s; **p. 175** silk organza rosettes and satin ribbon stocking bag (detail), circa mid 1940s; **p. 177** (top) chiffon evening gown (detail), circa mid 1960s, (bottom) silk taffeta and lace evening gown (detail), circa early 1960s; **p. 178** velvet vest worn as mini dress, circa late 1960s; **p. 179** velvet empire line evening gown, circa early 1960s; **p. 181** silk fitted mini cocktail dress with shell ornamentation, circa mid 1960s; **p. 182** velvet cheong sam style dress with hand embroidery (detail), circa 1960s; **p. 183** silk jacquard evening dress with self-covered buttons (detail), circa early 1930s; **p. 185** travelling ensemble of dress and matching long jacket with attached capelet, circa early 1930s; **p. 186** beaded and sequinned evening dress, circa early 1930s; **p. 188** silk crepe matelassé wedding gown (detail), circa late 1930s; **p. 189** beaded lambswool cardigan (detail), circa late 1950s; **p. 191** silk and metallic lamé opera coat with quilted collar, circa early 1920s; **p. 192** silk crepe wedding gown with rhinestone buttons (detail), circa early 1940s.

CREDITS

p. ix Brian Jenkins; **p. 5** Anidimi/Shutterstock; **p. 9** Everett Collection/Shutterstock; **p. 11** Everett Collection/Shutterstock; **p. 32** Peppersmint/Shutterstock; **p. 35** garanga/Shutterstock; **p. 45** Everett Collection/Shutterstock; **p. 47** Everett Collection/Shutterstock; **p. 49** Anton Oparin/Shutterstock; **p. 59** Everett Collection/Shutterstock; **p. 63** Everett Collection/Shutterstock; MJ Prototype/Shutterstock; **p. 71** Anton Oparin/Shutterstock; **p. 73** Karkas/Shutterstock; **p. 74** Iuliia Stepashova/Shutterstock; **p. 75** Everett Collection/Shutterstock; **p. 77** Everett Collection/Shutterstock; **pp. 78–9** Everett Collection/Shutterstock; **p. 87** Everett Collection/Shutterstock; **p. 100** Everett Collection/Shutterstock; **pp. 108–9** Larry Busacca/Getty Images; **p. 110** Terence Mendoza/Shutterstock; **p. 111** Everett Collection/Shutterstock; **pp. 120–1** Giorgios Kollidas/Shutterstock; **p. 127** Everett Collection/Shutterstock; **p. 132** Everett Collection/Shutterstock; **pp. 134–5** BonninStudio/Shutterstock; **p. 139** Everett Collection/Shutterstock; **pp. 142–3** Anton Oparin/Shutterstock; **p. 144** Gene Kornman/John Kobal Foundation/Getty Images; **p. 144** John Kobal Foundation/Getty Images; **p. 146** George Hurrell/John Kobal Foundation/Getty Images; **p. 147** Everett Collection/Shutterstock; **p. 148** both pics courtesy Featureflash/Shutterstock; **p. 152** Everett Collection/Shutterstock; **p. 158** lynea/Shutterstock; **p. 159** Everett Collection/Shutterstock; **pp. 160–1** AKaiser/Shutterstock; **pp. 185, 186** Everett Collection/Shutterstock; **p. 187** Bonnin Studio/Shutterstock.

INDEX

STYLE IS ETERNAL